A Traveller's Guide to the
SCOTLAND
of ROBERT THE BRUCE

A Traveller's Guide to the
SCOTLAND
of ROBERT THE BRUCE

Nigel Tranter & Michael Cyprien

ROUTLEDGE & KEGAN PAUL
London, Boston, Melbourne and Henley

CONTENTS

Introduction 5

The Featured Sites 7
*National map showing the location
of sites described in the gazetteer*

King Robert Bruce's Scotland 8–123
*A gazetteer to the sites
including the special articles listed below*

Weaponry and Armour 22
The Empty Throne 30
The Church's Part 54
Knighthood and Chivalry 66

Parliament and Government 78
The Burghs 92
Styles and Titles 100
Castles 110

The Rivals for the Throne 124
A family tree

A Pride of Bruces 126
A royal family tree

Further reading 128

First published in 1985 by Historical Times Incorporated,
2245 Kohn Road, Harrisburg, PA 17105, USA
and by Routledge & Kegan Paul plc
14 Leicester Square, London WC2H 7PH, England
9 Park Street, Boston, Mass. 02108, USA
464 St Kilda Road, Melbourne, Victoria 3004, Australia, and
Broadway House, Newton Road, Henley on Thames, Oxon RG9 1EN, England

Text by Nigel Tranter
Consultant Editor Dr Charles Kightly
Photography and Art Direction by Michael Cyprien

Printed in England by BAS Printers Limited,
Over Wallop, Stockbridge, Hampshire

ISBN 0 7102 0688 7

INTRODUCTION

Robert Bruce, Earl of Carrick and hero-king, was born at Turnberry Castle in Ayrshire in 1274, son of the fifth Lord of Annandale, who was of part-Norman ancestry, and of the Celtic Countess of Carrick in her own right. He ascended the throne he had fought for and grasped in 1306, and died in 1329. His was a strange life by any standards, for he grew up no hero – something of a playboy indeed, verging on the irresponsible. But he was brought to greatness by the needs of his native land – beaten down by that Hammer of the Scots, the megalomaniac Edward the First of England who coveted Scotland — and by the shining example of the great Scots patriot, William Wallace. So Bruce achieved his heroic stature in the hardest school, beginning his campaigns in a wholly foreign-occupied and garrisoned Scotland and fighting untrained against one of the most renowned militarists of that age: for Edward Plantagenet was originally known as the First Knight of Christendom, however much he forgot his knightly chivalry later.

In Bruce's long struggle to free his country, from 1297 until 1314's mighty victory at Bannockburn, he had to wage his warfare – in skirmish, ambush, pitched battle and of course often in flight and reverse and hiding – all over the face of Scotland, Highland as well as Lowland, from the Borders to Inverness and Ross, from Galloway to the Hebrides. To follow in his urgent footsteps, therefore, makes a fascinating and extensive pilgrimage. But – a word of warning!

I have heard it said that people change, and circumstances, but the land, the enduring land, does not. This is less than true, I fear. The land does change, and nothing is more certain than that Scotland has changed greatly since Bruce traversed it from end to end; and this has to be taken into account in any attempt to search out his tracks and traces, or confusion and disappointment will result. Many readers of my historical novels write to me, and quite a frequent complaint is that the scenes I describe therein are often almost unrecognisable when visited today by the said readers. This is scarcely my fault!

The first great difference to remember is modern drainage. This has transformed so much of the countryside and is often forgotten. In the old days, right up to the land-improvement era of the eighteenth and nineteenth centuries, practically no drainage was attempted by our ancestors. This meant a vitally different landscape, especially in a hilly and rainy country like Scotland. Much of the low ground was, in fact, flooded for at least part of the year, and was then impassable. It was overgrown with scrub-forest of hawthorn, birch, alder and elder, largely impenetrable and the haunt of wild animals, boar,

wolves, wildcats and of course deer by the thousand. The rivers were not confined or dyked and spread themselves, so lochs and pools and mires abounded. Cultivable land was scarce, and tended to be on the lower slopes of hills, where natural drainage took place, often on natural or contrived terracing. Land was seldom enclosed by any sort of fencing or walling, and fields were all but unknown, crops being grown on "rigs" or strip cultivation, with the use of the strips being switched around year by year so that various tenant cultivators got their chances of the better ground. Cattle – and Scotland was a cattle-country in the main, with sheep very secondary – grazed on common land, free to roam at will, so that herdsmen and shepherds formed quite a large part of the population. But the lack of tilled land made winter-feed for the beasts very scarce, and only the necessary breeding-stock could be maintained during the long winter months when there was little or no pasture. Each year's increase of stock therefore had to be sent away in the autumn, sold to the south, largely into England, in great herds or "droves"; and these went by recognised routes all over the land, "drove-roads", where the animals could graze at established resting-places overnight, on their months'-long journeys. These, then, were practically the only roads.

As a consequence of flooding and lack of drainage, these roads necessarily tended to follow the high ground, the ridges and firm terrain. Modern roads, on the contrary, seek to follow the lower routes where they can run more directly and avoid gradients: and this can greatly confuse the traveller seeking locations of past events. Moreover, bridges were few and far between, the normal means of crossing the many rivers and streams being by fords; and fords had to be at wide and shallow stretches, not at narrows suitable for bridging, another source of confusion today.

In Bruce's time, too, Scotland was largely covered in forest, and not only the Highlands by any means. Relics of the ancient Caledonian Forest remain here and there, open woodland mainly of Scots pine growing out of heather, bracken, bog-myrtle and cranberries, reaching high up towards the hilltops, again harbouring large numbers of wild animals. Admittedly the vast plantations of modern conifer forestry are again changing the landscape; but extensive as these are, they are as nothing to the original tree-grown scene.

Finally, of course, there is industrialisation, which requires no explanation but which can so drastically alter the picture, with factories, housing, slag-heaps, dumps, railways and the like making it difficult indeed to visualise the terrain as once it was.

Clearly, with all this in mind, to chronicle and describe any major proportion of the scenes and locations and sights visited by the Bruce, and actually or allegedly connected with his life and campaigns, would demand ten times the space here available. So I have had to limit myself to a significant and representative selection, bearing in mind the need for accessability by the visitor, the authenticity of the scene once reached, and the possibility of imaginative perception and reconstruction. The great majority of sites I have chosen, Bruce personally visited; but a few others have been included where the hero-king may not have been present, but where important events in his struggle took place, connected with his close associates.

Down the ages, of course, false links in the Bruce chain have been forged, some innocently by legend and contorted tradition, some less so – such as the tourist-trap "Bruce's Cave" convenient to the main road, for the credulous and car-bound sightseer. Such I have avoided – as I suggest, do you!

N.T.

Visiting the Sites
Most of the sites described in this book are freely accessible. If there is any question concerning access, it is always wise to ask permission of the landowner or occupier first. In any case, observe the country code with regard to gates, fences and walls, buildings and livestock. The Ordnance Survey Landranger maps are invaluable for finding some of the sites. The map numbers and the National Grid coordinates are included with the directions beside each entry.

1 Aberdeen
2 Aldcambus
3 Annan
4 Annandale
5 Arbroath
6 Isle of Arran
7 Auldearn
8 Ayr
9 Bannockburn
10 Berwick-on-Tweed
11 Pass of Brander
12 Brodick Castle
13 Buittle Castle
14 Caerlaverock Castle
15 Cambuskenneth Abbey
16 Cardross
17 Castle Tioram
18 Clackmannan
19 Closeburn Castle
20 Cumnock
21 Dalrigh
22 Dalswinton
23 Douglas
24 Dumfries
25 Dunaverty Castle
26 Dunfermline
27 Dunollie Castle
28 Dunstaffnage Castle
29 Ettrick Forest
30 Falkirk
31 Forfar
32 Glen Dochart
33 Glen Trool
34 Hawthornden Castle
35 Holyrood Abbey
36 Inchaffray Abbey
37 Inchmahome
38 Inchture
39 Inverurie
40 Irvine
41 Kildonan Castle
42 Kildrummy Castle
43 Lanark
44 Linlithgow
45 Loch Doon
46 Loch Lomond
47 Lochmaben
48 Loudoun Hill
49 Maybole
50 Melrose
51 Methven
52 Paisley
53 Peebles
54 Roslin
55 Rutherglen
56 St Andrews
57 Scone
58 Selkirk
59 Sliach
60 Stirling
61 Stobo
62 Stracathro
63 Tain
64 Tarbert Castle
65 Tor Wood
66 Turnberry Castle
67 Urquhart Castle
68 Whithorn

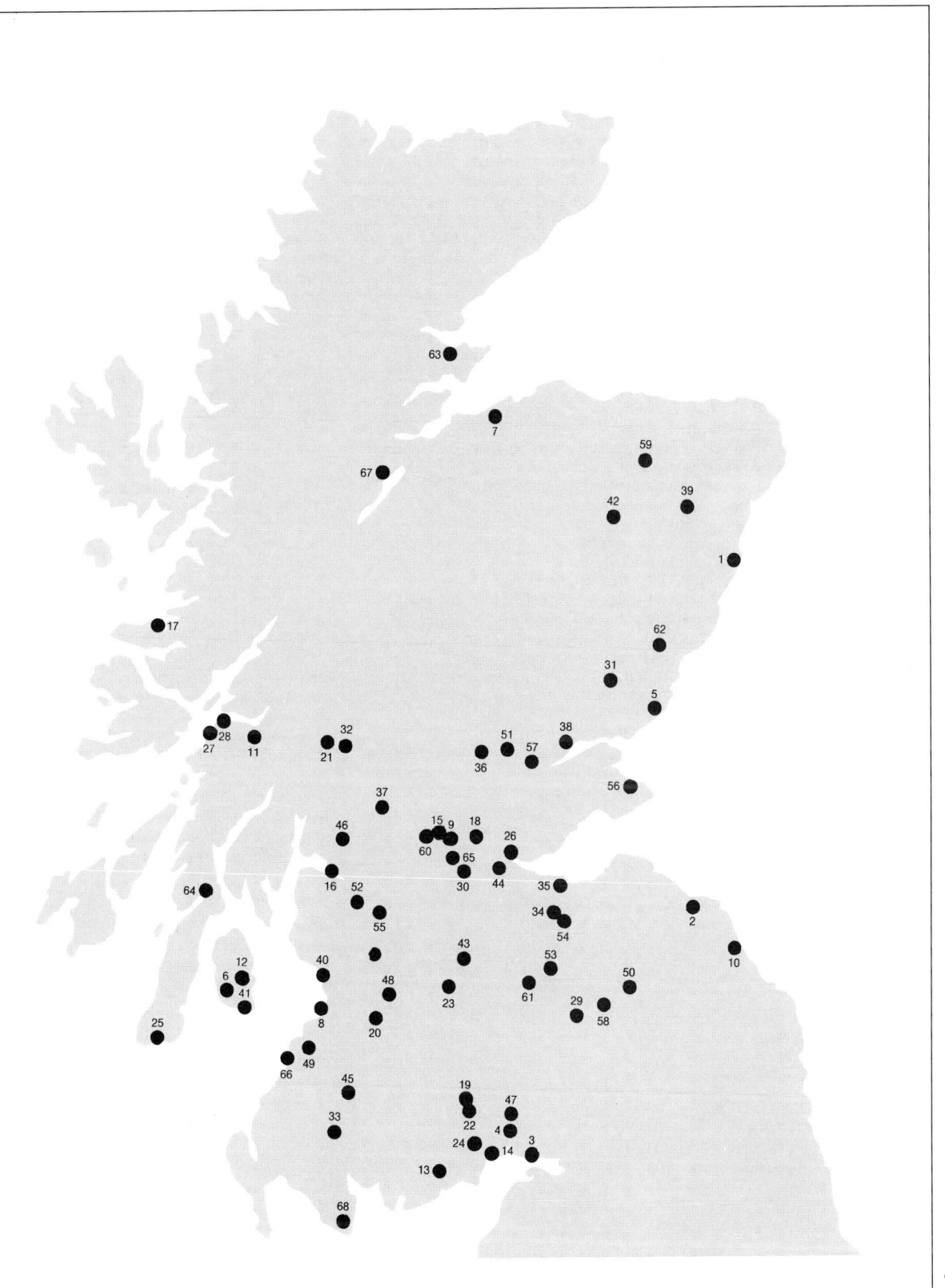

ABERDEEN Grampian
OS 38 NJ 930060

Aberdeen, "The Granite City", is on the north-east coast of Scotland, 125 miles north of Edinburgh via the A90, M90, A94 and A92.

The northern seaport and city of Aberdeen could not but feature quite largely in the Bruce story. King Edward stayed five days here in 1296, after the humiliation of King John Balliol at Stracathro; and in the next year, Wallace is reported by Blind Harry to have burned one hundred English vessels in the harbour – although this may well be something of an exaggeration. There is also a tradition that Bruce himself came to Aberdeen in 1306, immediately after the disaster of the Battle of Methven, so soon after his coronation – seeing his queen and his daughter on their way to hoped-for safety in Orkney, before himself returning to Argyll to continue the struggle and to sustain the second disaster of Dalrigh. But this is almost certainly a mistake. There would not be time between Methven and Dalrigh for this, and in the circumstances such a lengthy diversion would have been pointless.

However, the king was here in the following year. He was ill at Inverurie only fifteen miles away, and after he won his sick-bed victory in that vicinity, he held the first council of his reign at Aberdeen early in 1308. Aberdeen Castle was then still held by an English garrison, but in the following year it was besieged and reduced, although whether Bruce himself was present we do not know. In 1319 he conveyed to the burgh and community the royal forest of Stocket, plus valuable fishings on the rivers Dee and Don, in

a "great charter" from which the city dates its political institution.

Moreover, it should not be forgotten that Bruce had inherited the Lordship of the Garioch, a mere twenty miles or so from Aberdeen, as well as the earldom of Carrick. Also his sister Christian was Countess of Mar, which earldom's main seat was near Aberdeen at Kildrummy Castle, where the King's young daughter Marjory spent much of her childhood. So Bruce almost certainly would be a fairly frequent visitor to the Aberdeen area, even though records of his visits do not survive.

Aberdeen Castle has wholly disappeared, but it was sited where the municipal buildings now stand, in Union Street and Castle Street. And there is still a small Stocket Park northwards, in the vicinity of the Royal Infirmary, with Stocket Hill nearby. The Wallace Tower, so called because a statue of the great patriot graced it, now forms a splendid landmark on the Mote Hill at Tillydrone Road, having been removed and re-erected, stone by stone, from its original site in Nether Kirkgate. But although this tower is frequently reputed to have been the lodging of William Wallace, it is in fact a much later building, dating from the sixteenth century, whose true name is the Benholm Lodging. The old Brig o' Balgownie, built about 1320, was erected some say on the orders of King Robert, but others aver by Bishop Cheyne.

ALDCAMBUS Borders
OS 67 NT 805695

Aldcambus (also spelt Old Cambus) is situated on the A1107 some two miles south-east of Cockburnspath, where this road climbs from the A1 to the heights of Coldingham Moor.

This tiny North Berwickshire hamlet, seems a strange place to look for links with the hero-king. But he came here with his army in 1318, four years after Bannockburn, when Berwick-on-Tweed was still in English hands. He was on his way to attempt the recapture of that important town, port and castle. It is recorded that he halted at Aldcambus to build siege-engines from the timber growing here – interesting in that there is no woodland now. Presumably there was unlikely to be alternative supplies of wood nearer to Berwick. The present A1107 is on the line of the original route to Berwick and the Border, over Coldingham Moor's bleak heights, the present A1 highway down the Eye Water being a later development, made possible by drainage.

While the king was in this area, a monkish courier caught up with his force, bearing a let-

ter from the Pope ordering Bruce to agree to a truce with England, much to the Scots' disadvantage. Bruce, having been informed of the missive's contents, and determined to agree to no truce until he gained a formal peace-treaty with England (which the English consistently refused) would not open the sealed packet on the grounds that it was wrongly addressed, the superscription being "To Robert, Governor of Scotland" – Pope Boniface was rejecting his kingship. So the monk was sent away whence he came to get his letter properly addressed, and time was gained for the recapture of Berwick, which was indeed achieved shortly afterwards.

Aldcambus was formerly a deal larger than it is today, and was actually a parish, though its Norman church of St Helen on the cliff-top has since been swept away.

ANNAN Dumfries and Galloway
OS 85 NY 195665

Annan lies at the mouth of the river of the same name, on the A75, eight miles from the borderline at Gretna and sixteen miles east of Dumfries.

How frequently Bruce stayed at Annan is hard to say. After all, until he was twenty-one it was his grandfather's house, "the Competitor" not dying until 1295. Thereafter it was his father's seat, until 1304 – by which time the king-to-be, who seems to have been reared at his mother's castle of Turnberry, was more or less a footloose fugitive. So Annan, although the family seat, can have seen comparatively little of him. It was burned by the English, town as well as castle, in 1298, as a reprisal for his rising against Edward. He

ordered its rebuilding two years later but in his circumstances can have been seldom present.

However, the little red-stone town, with its views over the Solway Firth to the Lake District mountains, is inevitably much linked with his name; indeed the burgh's seal still displays the Bruce arms of a red saltire on gold. Oddly enough the place was more important *before* the king's time than after, even having a royal mint here in 1249, when his grandfather was cutting his wide swathe in Scotland. Perhaps the decline was not only because, before attaining the throne, the grandson's favourite seats were Turnberry and Lochmaben, but on account of less material influences. For in 1140 the famous Irish divine and mystic, St Malachy O'Moore, Bishop of Armagh and Papal Legate, cursed the house of Bruce and the town of Annan quite comprehensively. This was because its lord secretly hanged a robber for whom the said Bishop had interceded, he believed successfully – and clearly St Malachy was not the man to offend unnecessarily. Be that as it may, "the Competitor" lost his cause to John

Balliol, while Annan was burned in 1298, sacked in 1332, and burned again in 1542, and by 1609 it is recorded as too impoverished even to build itself a church – the inhabitants being forced to use the ruined castle as a place of worship. Who knows, the hero-king himself may have attributed some of his many misfortunes to the curse, including his belief that he had contracted leprosy, said to be "the finger of God upon him".

The site of the Bruce castle, of which the last traces were removed in 1875, is now the old churchyard.

The Bruces, originally called de Brus or de Brix from their ancestral home in Normandy, gained the important lordship of Annandale, in the shire of Dumfries, in about 1124: when one of the younger sons of the family (already settled in England, in Yorkshire) came north, like so many other young Normans, with King David the First of Scotland on his release from hostage-captivity at the English courts of William Rufus and Henry the First. This first Robert de Bruce of Annandale built castles at Annan town and at Lochmaben,

considerable traces of the latter being still to be seen. These early Bruces were, on the whole, not a notably spectacular family, although the fifth Robert, known as "the Competitor," foreshadowed his grandson's career by claiming the empty Scots throne after the death of the infant Maid of Norway, Alexander the Third's sole heir. His claim derived from his mother, Isabel, who was a great-granddaughter of the aforementioned David the First: and whose niece, the more famous Devorgilla, had married John Balliol

ANNANDALE Dumfries and Galloway OS 78 NY 070080
Annandale is a long and lovely valley reaching from salt-water at the Solway Firth nearly thirty miles up into the hills around Moffat and the famous features of The Devil's Beef Tub and the Grey Mare's Tail, with Lochmaben about halfway up. The vale is full of interest generally, quite apart from its links with Bruce. Well served with roads, it is threaded by the A74 the A701 and the B7020.

The lonely waters of the Ettrick Forest, ever the haunt of broken men in Scotland's long story.

of Barnard Castle, an Englishman, and helped him found Balliol College, Oxford. Devorgilla's son John Balliol, also claimed the Scots crown, and indeed won it by dubious means, which was to be the cause of much trial and sorrow thereafter. Bruce the Competitor's son, also Robert, was of different mettle, not ambitious for the throne. He went crusading to the Holy Land with a neighbour, Adam, Lord of Kilconquhar, and when his companion was killed, brought the sad news home to the widow – who was

Marjorie, Countess of Carrick in her own right, holder of a Celtic earldom descended from the ancient Lords of Galloway. Bruce promptly married the lady himself – or, as alleged, was hurried into matrimony by her, she very much taking the initiative, being a woman of considerable spirit by all accounts. Robert the hero-king was the offspring of the match, or the eldest of them, for he had four brothers and two sisters.
(*See* **Annan** and **Lochmaben.**)

ARBROATH Tayside
OS 54 NO 640410
Arbroath is on the east coast of Scotland, seventeen miles north-east of Dundee via the A92.

Arbroath and its great abbey will for ever be associated with one of the noblest documents of all time, the famous Declaration of Independence – debated, signed and sealed here in Bruce's presence, in 1320. Yet the place, largely because the abbey was one of the richest in Scotland, had other Bruce connections. Before his assumption of the crown, as one of the Guardians of the Realm, he required its abbot to pay the salary of the nation's Chancellor, or chief minister – Master Nicholas Balmyle – out of its large revenues. Later, when he nominated another cleric, his own chaplain and secretary Bernard de Linton, to be Chancellor, he actually appointed him Abbot of Arbroath as well. From time to time thereafter, as king, he

made donations of land to the abbey. And one of his last kingly acts, only a few days before his death, was to write to Edward the Third of England asking – now that there was a peace-treaty between himself and Edward – for the restoration of Haltwhistle church and lands, in Cumbria, given to Arbroath Abbey 150 years before.

But it is of course the renowned Declaration of 1320 for which the town and abbey are best known. This is one of the most stirring and significant affirmations of freedom the world has known. It was drawn up by the said Abbot Bernard, under Bruce's own supervision and guidance, for presentation to the then Pope (who was supporting the English) and was subscribed here by an

An example of thirteenth century multiple-arched arcading. Below, from left to right, the polygonal column base stands near to the centre of the great abbey church. A small doorway in the Early English style. The collapsed rose window at the west end of the abbey. Opposite page, Robert Bruce would have entered the abbey by this west door, still quite magnificent today. It was here that the famous Declaration of Independence was signed in 1320. Ruins require careful and constant maintainenace.

assembly of the earls, barons and land-holders of Scotland: it stressed their utter commitment to the ideal of freedom for all men, in government and in worship, and their resolution that if even King Robert himself were to attempt to deny them this essential freedom, they would forthwith expel him, as their enemy, and make another king to rule over them. "For so long as but one hundred of us remain alive . . ." On this tremendous averment the American Declaration of Independence is said largely to be based.

The ruined abbey stands proudly in red-stone magnificence just to the north-east of the old town centre, with King William the Lion (1165–1214) buried before the high altar – the same altar to which the Westminster Coronation Stone was brought by its abstractors on a spring morning in 1951, after its earlier removal from Westminster Abbey.

This was done after it had been decided that the stone must be brought to light again, in dignified fashion, in another abbey: and was performed under the secret but authoritative promise that the stone would thereafter remain in Scotland for at least a month "whilst tempers cooled". That it was carried back to London that same night, therefore, set Scotland in an uproar. The irony of it all was that this Westminster Stone is almost certainly not the true stone of Destiny (which Bruce on his deathbed, entrusted to the keeping of his friend Angus Og, Lord of the Isles, for safe-keeping in a secret place some-where in his Hebridean dominions) but a 700-year-old-fake.

The abbey is now in the care of the Department of the Environment and open to visitors.
See **Scone.**

ISLE OF ARRAN Strathclyde
OS 69 NS 960330

The Isle of Arran is a most worth-
while, indeed exciting place to visit for
anyone. It lies in the scenic Firth of
Clyde, ten miles from the nearest
point on the Ayrshire mainland coast.
The island is twenty miles long by half
that in width. It can be reached in two
ways – by Caledonian MacBrayne car
ferry from Ardrossan to Brodick
(fifteen miles); and by the smaller
northern car ferry from Claonaig, near
Skipness in Kintyre, to Lochranza
(only five miles).

This great island, lying in the Firth of Clyde and forming such a tremendous backcloth of dramatic mountains for the Renfrewshire and Ayrshire seaboard, has its significance for the Bruce story. For it was from here that the king, eleven months after his hasty coronation and the disasters which followed, launched his all but hopeless assault on his kingdom's occupied mainland, with only a tiny band of close companions and lieutenants. Arran was chosen because it was directly opposite Bruce's own Ayrshire castle and lands of Turnberry; and, although an English garrison held Brodick Castle, this was

not a large one and could not be reinforced at short notice. Moreover, the island was the territory of Bruce's kinsman and supporter, James, the High Steward, and its folk would be likely to be loyal and not betray their new monarch's presence, however forlorn seemed his chances of success.

At later stages of the struggle, Arran had its importance, largely geographically, since it all but dominated the sea approaches to Dumbarton, the greatest port in the west of Scotland.
See **Brodick**.

AULDEARN Highland
OS 27 NT 928555

Auldearn village lies on the A96, eight
miles west of Forres, where the B9101
branches off for Cawdor.

Of the former royal castle of Auldearn, near Nairn, no trace remains save for some grassy banks and mounds, representing foundations, on the higher ground of the old village of that name, beside the well-known seventeenth century doocote of Boath. Why there should have been another royal castle here, only two miles east of that at Nairn, is not clear. But it was here that William the Lion issued the second of his charters to Inverness, long before Bruce's day.

However, the hero-king's link with Auldearn ought not to be forgotten, for here he demonstrated, for his realm's sake, one of his finest exhibitions of mercy and forgiveness, qualities for which he was notable in a less-than-merciful age. For, in 1309, the king here accepted the surrender of William, Earl of Ross, the man who had so heartlessly betrayed Bruce's wife, daughter, and friends

to the English, after they had taken refuge in the sanctuary of St Duthac at Tain in Ross's territories, on their way to safety in Orkney after the disasters of Methven and Dalrigh. We all know the terrible fates of the betrayed. This was one of the most shameful deeds committed during that dire period, and so very personally against the monarch. Yet here, at Auldearn, Bruce accepted this powerful chief into his peace, for the well-being of his kingdom, and forced himself to pardon the perpetrator. Not only that, but he gave him back his forfeited lands, and the burgh of Dingwall in addition – this because he recognised how important was the great earl's adherence for the North.

Later, Sir Hugh Ross, the earl's son, married one of the King's sisters.
See **Tain**.

AYR Strathclyde
OS 70 NS 340220

Ayr lies on the south-west coast of
Scotland, thirty-three miles south-west
of Glasgow via the A77(T).

It is important to recognise how vital in the Wars of Independence was the south-western division of Scotland: much more so, indeed than any other part save the strategically-critical area around Stirling and the Forth crossing. This was largely because most of the main protagonists, on the Scots side, came from the south-west, with their armed forces – Wallace, Bruce, the Steward, Douglas, Randolph, Boyd and the rest; and because the area made a convenient invasion route into Scotland from Cumbria. Also Galloway, being partly the property of the Balliol-Comyn faction and partly Bruce's, was continuously fought over.

In all this south-western area, no single town was of more significance than Ayr, the county town of that great sheriffdom, with its port and castle. Here Wallace was confined in the old Tolbooth, now gone. Here, too, he made one of his first major assaults on the English, attacking the garrison of the castle and town in 1297. Here Bruce ordered the town to be burned down in the face of King Edward the First's advance after Wallace's defeat at Falkirk, in the next year. Bruce himself was Sheriff of Ayr in 1302, and in its port the English based a powerful fleet in 1306–7. From here, Aymer de Valence, Earl of Pem-

broke, rode out to be defeated by Bruce at nearby Loudoun Hill in 1307. The castle and town changed hands many times during the long struggle, and the citizens must have suffered greatly. In 1314 Ayr was garrisoned by Edward Bruce's army "of full seven thousand men and mair" preparatory to his expedition to Ireland, and a parliament was held here next year in the ancient St John the Baptist's church, when the King gave his reluctant consent to that Irish adventure. Likewise from Ayr, the year following, Bruce had to sail to the rescue of his headstrong brother. An earlier parliament had been held here in 1312.

Inevitably little remains to be seen of the Ayr of those far-off days. There is no trace of the castle, which was sited near the river-mouth beside the present Academy. The aforementioned St John's church stood where later Cromwell built his citadel. The Auld Brig, although often reputed to have been erected in the thirteenth century, was in fact not constructed until between 1470 and 1525. But Ayr is proud of its history, and Bruce and Wallace feature, with Robert Burns and others, in the stained glass of the Town Hall.

Above, landscape of Brown Carrick Hill. Bruce himself was Earl of Carrick in his mother's right. Left, the medieval arches and cutwaters of the Auld Brig of Ayr.

13

Bannockburn is two miles south of Stirling, via the A9 or the A905: the visitor centre is well signposted.

The Bruce statue at Bannockburn with his famous battle axe.

This is no place to enter into any description of one of the most famous battles of British history, its preliminaries, its tactics and strategy, its details and its consequences. A major book could be written on the subject; and numerous less-than-major works have considered it, described and analysed it. The location today is, of course, one of the most visited places in Scotland, beloved of tourists; and the publicity material on offer there is voluminous.

Unfortunately, what is usually described, and what the visitor is apt to see, however colourful, is somewhat misleading. For all the publicity, the show-place and commemora-tive exhibition (good as it is) along with the magnificent statue of the hero-king by Pilkington Jackson, is not placed where the real battle was fought, but on the high ground to the west where the Scots army *assembled* and where a preliminary skirmish took place. But the epic struggle, which was at last to free Scotland after eighteen years of occupation and almost continuous warfare, took place, of Bruce's deliberate intent, fully a mile to the east: on the low-lying flood plain of the Forth, the waterlogged area called "the Pows" (or pools), where the Pelstream Burn wound its muddy way to the great river, here beginning to widen a little into the estuary. So, after seeing all the publicity material and the statue, all very well worth viewing, those really interested in the battle itself should proceed on down to St Ninians, a village which has become a suburb of Stirling: and then back south-eastwards some little way, along the A9, to where a vista may be obtained of the low ground between that road and the meanderings of the Forth. All this land is now drained and dry, with the A905 crossing it, to Fallin and Grangemouth. But in 1314 it was sodden wilderness and bog, threaded by the Bannock and Pelstream and lesser burns, an extensive sump surrounding sundry islands of firmer ground; and as such it was the trap into which Bruce was determined to lure the vastly superior English army of Edward the Second.

The Plantagenet's magnificent force, usually numbered at about 80,000, not only vastly outnumbered the Scots, but was strong in heavy cavalry, (the equivalent of tanks today) and in archers (the equivalent of machine-gunners) Bruce had little of the first and less of the second, bows and arrows traditionally being for hunting, in Scotland, not for warfare. So he had somehow to seek to cancel out this superiority. And, as throughout his campaigns, he used the land brilliantly to aid him in this. Heavy chivalry, armoured knights on huge chargers themselves often weighed down with armour, were all but unstoppable – except on soft ground, into which their weight caused them to sink. And bowmen, with their deadly hail of arrows, could decimate a foe without ever themselves

coming under attack – unless they were more or less marooned in places where they could not bring their fire-power to bear. Hence the swamps for the cavalry and the islands to isolate the archers. Coaxing and luring them into these positions was the stroke of genius behind Bruce's strategy. The English were aware of all this, of course, and sought to avoid it. But so cunningly were the Scots forces used and distributed that they managed to decoy their powerful enemy into the very situation which the veteran English commanders must have recognised as highly dangerous. Edward the First, a born soldier whatever else, would never have let it get that far; but his son was a very different man. The cavalry floundered and sank, the bowmen were rendered ineffective, and more English died by drowning, trying to escape the massacre across the Forth, than were slain in the battle. Thus occurred one of the greatest victories and defeats of all time.

It is hard, today, to try to visualise the scene, with fertile farmlands, busy traffic, even a coal-mine distracting the imagination. But it is worth the effort.

The Bannockburn Memorial and Centre has its great interest of course, situated as it is at what was then the northern extremity of the great Tor Wood – which again helped Bruce in his assembly. It was also the scene of Bruce's renowned duel with Bohun, before the main battle. Here, in the Borestone area just west of the A9, two miles south of Stirling, is where the National Trust for Scotland seeks worthily to commemorate the event.

The ancient walled town of Berwick, where Northumberland meets Scotland, was in Bruce's time Scotland's greatest seaport, and inevitably entered into the Bruce saga importantly. Here, in 1296, Edward Plantagenet, at the very start of his campaign to take over the northern kingdom, wantonly slew allegedly 13,000 of its citizens, men, women and children, so that there was not one left alive who could not escape – this merely as an example to the rest of the nation as to what would be their fate should they seek to oppose the mighty invader. Not only that, but he is said to have forbidden the burial of the victims, ordering them to be left lying in the streets, the more eloquently to drive home his lesson. Today, Berwick's total population is less than 12,000.

And here, to its castle set high above the town – and so spared the smells and horror below – Edward ordered all Scotland's landholders to come and pay him homage for their lands, on pain of death, as Lord Paramount of Scotland, the title he adopted. Under the feudal system, such fealty-taking was necessary in law for the holding of landed property. So here came the young Robert Bruce, Earl of Carrick, along with the rest, to swear the hated fealty and sign the humbling list of the surrendered great ones of the

invaded kingdom, which Edward himself scornfully called his Ragman's Roll (a name which is said to be the origin of the word rigmarole). Surely one of the sorriest episodes in all Scotland's story.

Throughout the long Wars of Independence which followed, Berwick remained almost continuously in English hands, strongly fortified now and garrisoned, as the main staging-point for the many invasions of Scotland. It was in an open cage, hung from the castle walls here, that the Countess Isabel of Buchan, who had placed the crown on Bruce's brow at Scone in 1306, was held like an animal – day and night in all weathers – for folk to stare and jeer at, the price for contraverting King Edward of England. Not until 1318, four years after Bannockburn, did Bruce manage to retake the town and port, aided by some of its surviving citizens, notably one called Peter Spalding.

The impressive city walls which the visitor sees today are mainly later, of Elizabethan construction; but near the Tweedside and harbour, parts of the original Edwardian fortifications remain. Also tall fangs of masonry near the railway-station, readily seen from the train, mark the site of the castle on its cliff above the great river.

BERWICK-ON-TWEED
Borders
OS 7S NU 998530
Berwick-on-Tweed stands on the Anglo-Scottish border and the A1(T) road, sixty-seven miles north-west of Newcastle-upon-Tyne and fifty-eight miles east-south-east of Edinburgh.

15

The ruins of the old castle at Berwick run from the top of the town by the station, down a precipitous slope to the side of the river below where they are dominated today by the huge viaduct which spans the Tweed.

17

PASS OF BRANDER
Strathclyde
OS 50 NN 040293

The Pass of Brander begins just over ten miles east of Oban: the A85 from Oban to Perth traverses its entire length.

A steep and gloomy defile from which the River Awe runs out of Loch Awe to join Loch Etive, in central Argyll or Lorne, about ten miles east of Oban. The main A85 highway now threads the pass and gives a less daunting aspect to what must have been a fearsome place. The original track (no road) may well have been on the other, south, side of the river. Here, in 1308, Bruce, with the aid of his friend Sir Neil Campbell of Lochawe, won his first major Highland victory, ambushing John MacDougall of Lorn on his own doorstep, a powerful chief who had thrown in his lot with the English, and who had attacked the fleeing King at Dalrigh two years before, after the catastrophic Battle of Methven. At the Pass of Brander, Bruce learned how to use the land itself as his ally, a strategy which he was to perfect as time went on, utilising every feature, of cliff, broken terrain, river, swamp, hurtling rock and hidden cover, in his assault.

Some hillside climbing here is very worthwhile for the active investigator.

See **Dalrigh, Methven.**

BRODICK CASTLE Strathclyde
OS 69 NS 008380

Brodick Castle is a mile north of the terminus of the Isle of Arran car-ferry from mainland Ardrossan: the ferry takes an hour to reach Arran, and sails all the year round.

Brodick Castle, a splendid and imposing fortalice, latterly well-known as a seat of the Dukes of Hamilton and Montrose, stands on high ground a mile north of the shoreside village and ferry-terminal. At first sight it is a little difficult to distinguish the ancient from later

masonry, for all has been built in the same red sandstone and in a similar style of architecture; but closer inspection shows that the old part comprises the long main block lying east and west, three storeys and an attic in height, with walling topped by a parapet and

The crow-stepped gables and angle turrets of Brodick Castle are a typically Scottish feature.

walk. Most of this building belongs to the sixteenth and seventeenth centuries, but much older work is incorporated, dating from before Bruce's time. The castle is now in the care of the National Trust for Scotland and is open to visitors.

Obviously this fine stronghold must not be missed out on any visit to Arran. Yet its claim to a Bruce connection – it even boasts a "Bruce's Room" – is, in the present author's opinion, mistaken. Admittedly it had a minor part to play in the Wars of Independence, for it was garrisoned by the English invaders, since the island strategically dominated the Firth of Clyde and therefore the approaches to Dumbarton, the principal seaport of the West of Scotland. But the very fact of this English garrison militates against the claim that the castle could have sheltered the hero-king at a vital moment in his career.

The story is that here, in 1307, Bruce and his tiny band of close colleagues, after months of being hunted fugitives in the Highland West, returned and waited, in hiding, to embark on their great venture: – a landing on mainland Scotland again, to begin the campaign to purge the kingdom of the hated occupying forces. The tradition is that the king sent across the firth two trusted companions, who were secretly to spy out the land adjacent to his own birth-place castle of Turnberry, and were to light a beacon-fire at a selected spot, at Maidens, on a night when it seemed likely that the king could have an unopposed landing. In a lofty tower-chamber Bruce watched and waited. Unfortunately an accidental conflagration in the specified area brought the king and his band across before his scouts intended – however, the landing was effected and a measure of success followed, despite this misunderstanding.

There is no reason to disbelieve the substance of this tradition. But another version is that it was not Brodick Castle but Kildonan Castle in which Bruce waited – a much smaller place, isolated on a remote headland nine miles to the south, at the very tip of the island. This seems much more likely. For, since Brodick was the headquarters of John Hastings of Abergavenny, King Edward's governor, it was almost the last place Bruce would find refuge; and any glance at a contour map will show that the area on the Ayrshire coast from which he looked for the beacon-signal is in fact out of sight from Brodick, the land-masses of the Clauchland Hills and Holy Island intervening. Kildonan, on the other hand, looks directly across to Maidens and Turnberry, and, being a small eagle's-nest of a hold, it was just the sort of place for secret waiting. Moreover, it was a fortalice of a branch of Clan Donald of the Isles, whose chief Angus Og was of course a friend and supporter of the Bruce. Sir Walter Scott, I fear, is to be blamed for this discrepancy, for he it was who made Brodick the scene of the incident in his *Lord of the Isles*.

Kildonan still shows the shattered remains of a square cliff-top tower of the late thirteenth century, with six-feet-thick walling and three vaulted storeys, the upper having fallen in. Nevertheless it has (at hall-level) a mural garderobe with sanitary shute, quite a refinement for those days. A challenging place, it is built on the site of a Dalriadic fortress.

Did Bruce wait and watch in Brodick's tower, or, below, from the now ruined Kildonan Castle?

BUITTLE CASTLE Dumfries
and Galloway
OS 84 NX 819617
*The castle mound is reached from
Dalbeattie by taking the A711 and
then the A745 towards Castle
Douglas, and turning northwards (or
right) off the A745 at a sharp bend
about a mile outside Dalbeattie: this is
the minor road to Buittle Place, and
the castle is east of the Place, in a field
by the River Urr.*

Buittle (pronounced Bittle) is today a relatively unimportant Kirkcudbrightshire parish, only a few miles north of the Solway Firth, lying between Castle Douglas and Dalbeattie, in the very attractive valley of the River Urr, known sometimes as the Trossachs of Galloway. There is no town nor even village of the name now; but Buittle was mightily important in the Scotland of Bruce's time, and indeed long before that. For here was the great castle which constituted the principal seat of the ancient Celtic Lords of Galloway, and as such it came to John Balliol when that illustrious line ended in the famous heiress Devorgilla. She, of course, had married the English Balliol of Barnard Castle, and had founded Balliol College, Oxford in memory of her husband and also Sweetheart Abbey, some ten miles north-east of Buittle, for her body to lie with his. So her son, John Balliol (whom King Edward of England, as adjudicator, chose to become King of Scots) inherited Buittle Castle along with the lordship of Galloway. It became one of the most fought-over strongholds of Scotland.

Today little remains of the castle itself other than grass-grown mounds, a few traces of masonry and a well, at a bend in the River Urr about a mile north-west of Dalbeattie. But the position is notable and worth visiting. It is not to be confused with the nearby Buittle Place, which is its late sixteenth century successor, now a farmhouse and much altered, and said to have been built largely out of the stones of the original castle.

Buittle, because of its strong position and being the headquarters of the Galloway lordship, was early involved in the tug-of-war for the crown of Scotland, even before the death of the Maid of Norway in 1290. For Bruce's grandfather, Lord of Annandale and known

as "the Competitor," was a descendant of Devorgilla's aunt Isabel, niece of King William the Lion, and thus claimed to be next heir to the child Margaret of Norway; and when John Balliol did likewise, he seized Balliol's castle of Buittle in 1286. Balliol got it back, of course, when he became king in 1292; but when he was himself deposed by the Hammer of the Scots, Buittle was, like so many other Scots strongholds, taken over and garrisoned by the English. It remained in their hands long after most of the others had fallen to the Scots in the Wars of Independence. Even in 1309, when Bruce, now king, made his brother Edward Lord of Galloway, it managed to hold out against that Edward's attacks; and it was not until King Robert himself came to besiege it in 1313, not long before Bannockburn, that it finally fell. The reason for its ability to resist assault, as well as its own strength and position, was the fact that it stood only some four miles from Palnackie, the port of Castle Douglas, on the Rough Firth, a branch of the Solway, and thus could easily be reinforced and provisioned from the English Solway coast. So battles and skirmishes a-many must have taken place in this attractive valley.

After Edward Bruce's death in Ireland in 1318, without legitimate heir, the king gave Buittle to his friend, "the Good" Sir James Douglas; and the lands remained with that family until passing to the Maxwells in the sixteenth century, when the existing Place was built.

Of interest nearby to the south, near Buittle Bridge, are the great granite quarries of Craig Nair, which used to employ hundreds of labourers and from which the granite for the Thames Embankment and Liverpool Docks was obtained.

*Above, follow the signpost at Buittle Bridge for the single
track road to the right near the top of the hill.*

Left and top, the overgrown ruins are on private land and permission to visit them should be sought from the helpful owners of Buittle Place. Above, the River Urr at Buittle Bridge.

Weaponry and Armour

The arms and armour in use at the time of the Wars of Independence deserve some consideration. There was no great range of weaponry, and such as there was varied between that used by mounted knights and that used by men-at-arms. Artillery was extremely primitive at this stage, and little of it was available to the Scots anyway, who of course were more inclined to guerilla-type warfare in which cannon and heavy siege-machinery would have been only an encumbrance. It is worth remembering, too, that there was little tradition of archery in warfare in Scotland, whereas in England and Wales the good yew bow and clothyard shaft were vastly important; which situation greatly disadvantaged the Scots, who looked on archery as an adjunct of hunting rather than war. Cross-bows were also used, but not commonly.

The following personal weapons were carried by knights and mounted men. Swords were very large and long, two-handed as to hilt, and often almost as tall as their wearers. They were carried down the back, and when brought into use, reached for over the head with both hands and brought over and down with great force. A stroke from such swords could cut off a limb, or the head from the body. But they were unhandy things to wield and demanded very strong wrists; and cut-and-thrust, as with smaller swords, was all but impossible. During close in-fighting these great swords were of little use, and the dirk or dagger was used. Battle-axes

were favoured by some, and Bruce himself was an acknowledged expert in the use of these weapons, his worsting of Bohun, in the famous bout before Bannockburn, being with a battle-axe. Axes were either single or double bladed, with a shaft short enough to allow swift changes of thrust and direction. Maces were also used by mounted men, these being really clubs consisting of a shaft topped by a heavy spiked ball of iron, either fixed or on a short chain, useful against armour and steel helmets. Lances were likewise carried by knights and cavalry.

The foot, or infantry, were otherwise equipped. They had shorter, stabbing swords, and also long spears and pikes, sometimes of very great length, which although unwieldy also were useful in the formation of "hedgehog" defensive squares. Halberds, spears with an axe-head on a long shaft, were also used.

Armour varied greatly. At this period plate-armour, with jointed arm and knee-pieces, was little seen, and chain-mail shirts, belted, were usual with knights, sometimes having chain hoods. Helmets were open, usually lacking the later visors, although some had a fixed covering for the face. They were frequently topped with heraldic coloured plumes for identification. Also to establish identity, most important in a set battle, lords and knights wore linen surcoats over their armour, emblazoned in colours with their heraldic devices or "coat-of-arms" (this being the origin of the phrase): these devices were repeated on their long shields. Standards, banners and pennons also indicated identity, for friend and foe alike. Horses likewise could be armoured, but the weight of this tended to demand heavy beasts as chargers ("destriers" as they were called) which were beloved of the English chivalry but little seen among the Scots. These heavily-armoured horses and their knightly riders acted almost like tanks in modern warfare; but they had the great disadvantage of being so weighty that they were slow and unmanoeuvreable and could sink into soft ground – hence the Scots tactics of seeking to lure the enemy into marshy terrain wherever possible.

As well as elementary cannon and mortars, awkward to transport and usually drawn by slow teams of oxen, siege weaponry could consist of various contraptions such as sows (or movable sheds to protect the users of battering-rams) mangonels for throwing great stones, trebuchets which were similar catapults, balistas for slinging projectiles, and beaked rams for pecking at masonry and castle walls.

In the field, caltrops were a device (allegedly invented in Scotland) for use against advancing cavalry. These were of forged iron, with four spikes so contrived that however they were thrown down one spike always stood upright. Sown liberally on ground over which the enemy were to charge, they could have a devastating effect on the horses' hooves. But because of the necessity for sufficient numbers, and non-availability, they were little used in guerilla warfare. Fire-arrows were employed against the thatched roofs of houses, to great effect. Therefore castles and tower-houses were never thatched, stone slates being preferred.

Where the common folk were fighting for their lives and homes, of course, all sorts of non-military implements were used as weapons – hatchets, clubs, flailing-chains, sticks and stones.

CAERLAVEROCK CASTLE
Dumfries and Galloway
OS 84 NX 026656

The castle is six miles south-east of Dumfries, by the B725.

This undoubtedly is one of the most spectacular castles in Scotland, rising out of flooded marshland some six miles south-by-east of Dumfries, on the edge of the Solway flats, in a most obviously defensive site. In attractive pink stone masonry, it is of most unusual design, for Scotland, being triangular in plan – this no doubt being largely dictated by the nature of the islanded site; but it is also very ambitious architecturally, with much stone carving, elaborate corbelling and heraldic decoration. The apex of the triangle consists of great twin drum-towers flanking the portcullis and drawbridge entrance, backing on to a massive keep which also does duty as a gatehouse. High curtain-walls, formerly topped by parapet-walks, stretch back southwards, to enclose a courtyard; and against these, handsome subsidiary buildings have been erected at various periods, with a tall palace-block added on the east side in the seventeenth century. Circular flanking-towers at the other two angles of the triangle complete the lay-out. The building, on its island in the waterlogged marsh, is ruinous, but well-maintained in the care of the Department of the Environment.

The site has always been an eminently defensive one, and it is believed that even the Romans had a station here. But the first recorded stronghold dated from 1220, being a seat of the Maxwell family, who had come to the South-West from Roxburghshire. During the Wars of Independence it was inevitably important, dominating the fords and channels of the Solway as it did. William Wallace occupied it in 1296, briefly. And in 1300, King Edward Plantagenet himself came to besiege it, with 3,000 troops. Sir Eustace Maxwell and his sixty men held out for two days. Thereafter Caerlaverock remained garrisoned by the English until 1312, when Bruce recaptured it and reinstalled Sir Eustace. But recognising the danger of strong castles falling into enemy hands and then serving as bases, the king largely dismantled it. It was rebuilt after Bruce's death, and in 1347 Sir Eustace's son Herbert switched allegiance to Edward Balliol and the English cause. The Scots loyal to Bruce's son David the Second had to retake it, and this time it was thoroughly demolished.

By 1425 the Maxwells had returned to their loyalty, and were back to begin the building of the present castle. Since the Wardenship of the West March became more or less hereditary in the Lords Maxwell, Caerlaverock was established as the West March seat of government, and as such was the scene of much stirring activity. Here, soon after its completion, was confined Murdoch, Duke of Albany, James the First's ambitious cousin, before his execution for high treason; and the south-west flanking tower is still called Murdoch's. Here too came James the Fifth in 1542, at the time of the Rout of Solway Moss nearby, after which disaster the shattered monarch retired to Falkland to die,

leaving the throne to the week-old Mary Queen of Scots. The castle was later held for his great-grandson, Charles the First, by the Maxwell first Earl of Nithsdale, who defied the covenanting forces for no less than thirteen weeks. After its battering on that occasion, Caerlaverock was never again restored.

An interesting Bruce connection was the king's order that £5 yearly, then quite a substantial sum, should be levied on Caerlaverock for the upkeep of the Chapel of the Holy Rood at Dumfries, which his sister Christian had founded in memory of her husband Sir Christopher Seton, whom King Edward had hanged at that town – this when the aforementioned Sir Eustace Maxwell made a temporary allegiance to England, as his son was to repeat later. So Caerlaverock has seen treachery as well as heroism, shame as well as honour.

Far left, an intruder's view of one of Caerlaverock's round towers. From the gaps between the stone corbels (upon which a wooden staging once rested), the defenders would have dropped missiles upon the unfortunate attacker below. Above, this impressive stronghold was built, to replace an earlier castle nearby. Left, an aspect of the well-preserved ruin showing the defensive ramparts surrounding the moat.

CAMBUSKENNETH ABBEY
Central
OS 57 NS 809940

Cambuskenneth Abbey stands just to the east of Stirling, by the River Forth: it is reached by a signposted side road off the A907 main road from Stirling to Alloa and Dundee.

Stirling was without doubt the most significant location in all old Scotland, both on account of its position and its possession of the most powerful and secure royal fortress in the kingdom. Here, where Highlands and Lowlands join, and the wide arm of the sea, the Firth of Forth, suddenly narrows sufficiently to be bridged, almost in the centre of Scotland, the towering castle-rock frowns over all. Here history was made, more dramatically than almost anywhere else in the land. And here, just across the extraordinary windings of the River Forth, lies Cambuskenneth Abbey. Inevitably it was involved in much of the making of that history.

The site is almost an island one, set in one of the remarkable loops created by the river's meanders. Before modern land-drainage was put in hand, it must have been almost unreachable, unless its abbots co-operated; nowadays access is readily gained from the A907 Alloa-Stirling highway and by a short side-road. This comparative invulnerability was highly important and necessary in times past, for mighty battles were fought on the abbey's very doorstep – Stirling Bridge one mile to the north-west and Bannockburn one mile to the south, as well as other lesser conflicts.

Bruce was not present at Stirling Bridge – that was William Wallace's triumph. But after the still more significant victory of Bannockburn, it was to Cambuskenneth that the King came, on the 25th of June 1314, to give thanks, to mourn his dead, to receive the surrender of a host of lordly and knightly English captives, and to consider the vast amount of booty and riches which had fallen into Scots

hands. It is also interesting that here, in 1308, Sir Neil Campbell of Lochawe, Sir Gilbert Hay of Erroll and others of Bruce's close companions, swore a vow before the high altar to defend to the death the title of Bruce to the Scottish crown – this when the fugitive king's fortunes were at a low ebb, just before the Battle of the Pass of Brander. Here, still earlier, in 1304, before he was king, Bruce and Bishop Lamberton entered into a secret bond of mutual friendship and alliance against all men, the same year that King Edward the First was at Cambuskenneth. And here, in 1326, the king held one of his last parliaments. So few places could have been more important for Robert the Bruce.

The name means the Field of Kenneth, scene of a still earlier battle waged by one of the Celtic kings of that name. The abbey was founded in 1147, one of David the First's many monastic institutions, and given to the Augustinian Order, the Black Canons. Its abbots frequently attained great prominence in the land, being so close to the seat of royal power. Abbot Henry, in 1493, was Lord High Treasurer; Abbot Patrick Paniter, Secretary to James the Fourth, was ambassador to France; Abbot Alexander Mylne was a noted scholar, another ambassador to various countries and instigator and first President of the Court of Session, in 1532; and Abbot David Paniter, the last before the Reformation, was Secretary of State. James the Third and his queen are buried here, not far from the place where he died, after the Battle of Sauchieburn in 1488.

The abbey is now in the care of the Department of the Environment.

A lofty square tower overlooks the extensive remains of the abbey seen here and on the page opposite.

Climb to the top of the tower to see this good collection of sculptured fragments.

CARDROSS Strathclyde
OS 63 NS 345775

Cardross village is three miles west of Dumbarton, via the A814: but the site suggested here as Bruce's last home is immediately north of the Dumbarton suburb of Brucehill, in the fields by the River Leven at NS 390765.

There are at least two Cardrosses in Scotland, not very far apart – after all, the name in Gaelic just means the curved headland. The one connected with Robert Bruce lies just west of the town of Dumbarton, at the widening of the River Clyde to its estuary. There is a village of that name, three miles west of Dumbarton, but this is comparatively modern. The situation of Bruce's last home is much nearer the town, although exactly where is uncertain, for nothing remains of the building. Traditionally it was at what is now called Castlehill, an eminence in a western suburb; but almost certainly this is a mistake. There *is* what appears to be the site of a motte-and-bailey castle at Castlehill; but it is known that Bruce's house was no castle but an unfortified manor-house; also it is known that this royal residence was close to salt-water, where the king kept ships, and there is recorded an occasion when his ship was drawn up into the burn beside the house. So clearly this must have been down beside the confluence of the River Leven and the Firth of Clyde, and probably where the Dalmoak Burn enters the river. It is a pity that this so important site should be unmarked; for here the hero-king chose to spend the last three years of his life and here he died in 1329. The place should be a national shrine.

His choice of Cardross to (as it were) retire to, at the age of fifty-five, worn out by the desperately hard life he had been forced to live, is strange. He had, of course, destroyed nearly all the royal castles, deliberately. But not Dumbarton Castle itself. Yet he did not

elect to live there, choosing instead this modest establishment nearby, with nothing of defence nor fortification about it, as though he desired to be done with warlike things. And it is worthy of note that he did not retire to his own calf-country of Ayrshire or Annandale, but to this Gaelic-speaking area on the edge of the Highland West. Dumbarton (or Alclyd) of course, was the ancient capital of the former Celtic kingdom of Strathclyde, and so had historic significance as well as being the focal point for all practical sea-links with the south-west, the Hebrides, the Highland seaboard and likewise Ireland. Also, in his later years, Bruce had developed a major interest in ships and sailing, no doubt recognising how greatly the Scots cause would have been served had he possessed a naval strength, as did the English – a fact his friend Angus Og of the Isles would be sure to emphasise. At any rate, here at Cardross, although a sick man suffering probably from dropsy as well as other ailments, he was able to enjoy a little of the peace which had so eluded him all his days, while still ruling his realm with a sure hand – and indeed negotiating the final peace-treaty with England, which was signed only the year before he died.

A visit to Dumbarton and Cardross may not reveal much which dates from Bruce's day, in man-made things; but the great castle-rock, the River Leven, the Clyde estuary and all the blue Highland mountains, are the same – and it was these which the king chose as the last things on which to feast his eyes.

CASTLE TIORAM Highland
OS 40 NM 662725

Castle Tioram stands on a tidal islet at the head of Loch Moidart on the Highland west coast, and can be reached, on foot only, at low tide. From Fort William, travel to Ardmolich (the nearest hamlet) via the A830 and A861 westwards, through Glenfinnan and Lochailort: or southward on the A82 to Corran Ferry, then westward on the A861 through Glen Tarbert, Strontian and Acharacle to Ardmolich.

Where Robert Bruce spent the months after his defeat at Methven in June 1306, until his return to mainland Carrick in February 1307, is one of the mysteries of history. There is no sure record. We know that he fled from the ambush at Dalrigh to Loch Lomond, then to the royal castle of Dunaverty in Kintyre before crossing to Rathlin Island off the Irish coast. But after that various chroniclers give differing suggestions. Ireland itself, Orkney, even Norway, as well as the Hebrides, are put forward. Fordoun, reasonably accurate usually and writing at the end of the same century, declares that he survived by God's mercy and the help of Christina of the Isles. Certainly afterwards Christina MacRuari proved the King's good friend. She was the daughter and heiress of Alan MacRuari MacDonald, Lord of Garmoran, a descendant of the great Somerled of the Isles, and had been married to Donald of Mar, a younger brother of the Earl of Mar – therefore a brother of Bruce's first wife, Isabel of Mar. So there was a family connection. Christina had inherited great possessions in the Hebrides and West Highland seaboard. But Garmoran was her main lordship and Castle Tioram in Moidart was its principal seat. It seems probable, therefore, that Bruce passed at least some of these months at this remote castle, for almost cer-

tainly he was not in Orkney, much less Norway. During the period, he sent secret messengers to collect his earldom of Carrick rents, at the Martinmas (November) term, so he cannot have been so very far away from the Ayrshire coast; and of course he himself landed there the following February, to commence his campaign of recovering his kingdom. From Orkney or Norway he would have been likely to land on the east side of the country, where he had support in Moray and Aberdeenshire. So Garmoran fits the case.

Castle Tioram, although ruinous, still looks the romantic stronghold of a Highland chief. It rears itself on a small tidal island in the mouth of Loch Moidart, which lies just north of the Ardnamurchan peninsula, the most westerly point of mainland Britain, and south of Arisaig. The castle can be walked out to over the sands at half-tide. Although much of the building dates from the late sixteenth century, the original eight feet thick curtain-walling survives, built by Somerled himself in the twelfth century, enclosing the later keep and turrets. Apart from this the castle must be much as it appeared in Bruce's day. Later it became the seat of the chiefs of Clanranald, successors of the MacRuaris; and here the unfortunate Lady Grange was imprisoned by her judge husband in 1732.

In less than thirty minutes, the incoming tide severes the castle's sandy link with the mainland. It was the seat of Christina of the Isles, of Clanranald descent.

29

The Empty Throne

When Alexander the Third, King of Scots, fell to his death over the cliff at Kinghorn in Fife, one stormy night in March 1286, he left Scotland on the horns of a dilemma indeed, for there was no obvious male heir. In fact, there were grave doubts about any heir at all, since there was neither experience nor tradition of a *Queen* of Scots, and many of the realm's magnates held that it was not only undesirable but also unconstitutional for a female to sit on the throne. Scotland had always needed a strong king: and the only direct living descendant of Alexander was his granddaughter, the infant Maid of Norway—the child of his daughter Margaret, who had married the young King Eric of Norway. A more improbable monarch for Scotland than this foreign baby would be hard to contemplate. Alexander had fathered three other children by his first wife, Margaret daughter of Henry the Third of England, but they and she had all died. He had no brothers nor near kin.

But even so there was a complication. Alexander had remarried only months before his tragic death, his new wife being the beautiful Yolande de Dreux, from France. And she might be pregnant. Should she bear a child, this infant would supersede the little Norwegian princess in the succession. So there had to be a nail-biting wait, for the necessary months, to see if Queen Yolande produced offspring. In the event she did not, and she was packed off back to France, the Maid of Norway being sent for to mount the throne; although this was much against the wishes of some of the most powerful nobles in the land, in especial the heads of the great families of Bruce and Balliol.

Years before, when King Alexander's father, Alexander the Second, had as yet produced no offspring, and there was similarly no heir to the throne, it had been decided that in the event of none being born, the succession must fall to the descendants of David the First, David being the youngest son of King Malcolm Canmore and St Margaret. David's grandson, David, Earl of Huntingdon, had left four children, a son and three daughters. The son died young, but the daughters had all survived and married, with offspring. Of these the principal claims now came from the Bruce and Balliol families. The eldest daughter, Margaret, had married the Lord of Galloway and produced the famous Devorgilla, who herself wed an English lord, John Balliol of Barnard Castle, their son being another John Balliol. While Isabel, the next sister, had married Sir Robert Bruce, fourth Lord of Annandale, and produced another Robert, fifth Lord – the grandfather of the hero-king. The third sister, Ada, married an Englishman, named Hastings.

Then, in September 1290, the delicate Maid of Norway, on her way over to Scotland to mount the throne, fell ill and died in Orkney, to the consternation of all.

So now there was the great question to be decided of who should succeed to the throne. John Balliol was the grandson of the eldest of King David's great-granddaughters, Margaret; but Robert Bruce, fifth Lord of Annandale, was a generation nearer, the son of the second sister, Isabel. Who had the better right? Vehement, indeed warlike, were the claims as to which had priority. And, since the crown was, as it were, up for grabs, sundry other claimants (including John Hastings, grandson of the other sister Ada) put in for it. Civil war threatened.

In this extraordinary situation King Edward the First of England saw his opportunity. He was, of course, the son of Henry the Third and therefore had been brother-in-law of the dead Alexander. A great warrior and known as "The First Knight of Christendom," he was able and shrewd, but power-hungry. And he wanted Scotland. He offered to act as adjudicator and honest broker in a "Competition" for the Scots throne, to decide on whose claim was best; but in return for this service demanded that he himself should be acknowledged by the winning claimant as overlord or Lord Paramount of the northern kingdom. Whether this arrogant claim was ever fully accepted by the said "Competitors," or could have had any validity even it it had been, is a matter for debate. But the Competition went on, and in due course, not unnaturally, Edward found in favour of the claimant with the weakest character, John Balliol, to the fury of the Bruce faction. So Balliol became King John of Scots, the first and last of that name. Duly, at first, Balliol paid some sort of allegiance to the English monarch, but later threw this off when Edward treated him like some mere vassal, ordering him down to London on the most minor of charges and hectoring him before all the court there. When even this worm turned, Edward declared that the Scots had now no king but himself, and marched north with a great army, to unseat the wretched Balliol and send him into exile in France. He then proceeded to occupy the castles and fortresses of Scotland.

The Wars of Independence followed, with the heroic William Wallace coming quickly into the lead, and showing the way for the young Robert Bruce – grandson of the "Competitor," the fifth Lord of Annandale, and Earl of Carrick in the right of his Celtic mother. After years of warfare, Robert Bruce assumed the throne in 1306.

CLACKMANNAN Central
OS 58 NO 910920

The little town of Clackmannan stands on a ridge of rising ground above the levels of the Carse of Forth, three miles east-south-east of Alloa, on the A907, and eight miles east of Stirling.

This ancient little town, not much more than a village, which gives its name to the smallest county in Scotland, may or may not qualify fully for inclusion herein, since the author has discovered no actual record of Robert the Bruce's activities there. Almost certainly, however, he would have visited it, possibly quite frequently, for it was at the centre of a royal forest: it also undoubtedly has Bruce family connections, while there is a long-standing local tradition that the hero-king built Clackmannan Tower. This last seems not very likely however; since the style of architecture is typically fifteenth century, not late thirteenth or early fourteenth, although there seems to have been an earlier stronghold on the site. Just adjoining, formerly stood an old mansion which was long the seat of the lineal descendants of another Robert Bruce, kin to King Robert, to whom David the Second, Bruce's son, gave the castle and barony of Clackmannan in 1359. In this house was long preserved the great two-handed sword, also the helmet, of King Robert. And, interestingly, therein the last laird's widow, Mrs Henry Bruce of Clackmannan, on the 26th of August 1787, "knighted" with this sword Scotland's famous poet Robert Burns. The relics thereafter passed into the keeping of the Earls of Elgin and Kincardine, present heads of the Bruce family. The estate had remained in Bruce hands, therefore, from 1359 to 1796.

In the centre of Clackmannan's broad main street stands the Old Tolbooth or townhouse, an attractive feature of burgh architecture; with beside it not only the early market-cross on its plinth but a remarkable monolith,

a tall standing-stone known as the Stone of Manau or Mannan, from which the town and county take their name. There can be few counties, parishes or even towns which are named for a single standing-stone. Just who this Manau was is not absolutely certain; but it is thought that he was the same Manannan MacLir of Irish legend who gave his name to the Isle of Man.

The fortalice aforementioned stands higher on the ridge dominating the town, a fine double-tower seventy-nine feet high, a prominent landmark for miles around. The lower half of the north tower does seem to date from the fourteenth century; but whether Robert the Bruce built it is another matter, for his policy was always to demolish stone castles rather than erect them. The south tower is crowned at parapet-level by a belfry and a beacon-brazier, this last for a signal or warning fire. It was claimed that this beacon, lit, could be seen by at least seven other Bruce castles.

Thomas Bruce, a "near relative" of the king, aided the High Steward, later Robert the Second, in a rising against Edward Balliol and the occupying English power, in Ayrshire in 1334, and as a reward was given part of the crown hunting-forest of Clackmannan, his descendants holding the hereditary office of Foresters and Sheriffs of Clackmannan. From them are descended the Earl of Elgin and Kincardine and the Lord Balfour of Burleigh. The nearby estate of Kennet is still a Bruce possession, the owner being the twelfth Lord Balfour of Burleigh, who in fact bears the name of Robert Bruce.

CLOSEBURN CASTLE
Dumfries and Galloway
OS 78 NY 908922

Closeburn Castle is about a mile east of Closeburn village, which is thirteen miles north-north-west of Dumfries, via the A76(T): the castle is reached by a side turning off the A76.

This is probably one of the oldest inhabited houses in Scotland, and, comparatively unaltered, it retains its aspect of antiquity and massive strength. The exact date of its erection is unknown, but it bears all the indications of belonging to the fourteenth century – which very few surviving Scottish castles do. A tall square keep, without ornamentation but with walls reaching ten to twelve feet in thickness, it stands a mile east of the village of Closeburn – which in fact should be Kilosburne, the church of Osbern or Osburne, presumably an early missionary saint. It is built on a slight eminence which was formerly an island in a loch, now drained, and is unusual in that three of its storeys are stone-vaulted, the basement, first and top floors.

Although Bruce himself must often have visited Closeburn, I have seen no records of this. But its lairds were important vassals of the Bruce Lords of Annandale; and the castle is no great distance from the Bruce seats of Annan and Lochmaben. The Kirkpatrick family are traditionally said to have been in possession of these lands from as early as the ninth century; but the first recorded reference to them is when an Ivone de Kirkpatrick

witnessed a charter of David the First to Robert de Brus, first Lord of Annandale, undated but before 1141. In 1232 King Alexander the Second confirmed in possession another Ivone; and the Kirkpatricks remained the lairds until 1783 – although the estate was taken from Stephen Kirkpatrick, father of Sir Roger, a Bruce supporter, by Edward the First of England and given to one of his own people, John Cromwell. The Kirkpatricks won it back, of course.

The most renowned story connected with Closeburn is the 'mak siccar' incident. This was when Bruce, on hearing of the Red Comyn's treachery in betraying him and his plans to Edward Plantagenet, stabbed the Comyn before the altar of the church of the Greyfriars at Dumfries; and coming out of the building, himself appalled at what he had done in a fit of fury, confessed to his waiting supporters that he feared that he had slain the Comyn. Sir Roger de Kirkpatrick then declared that he would "mak siccar", that is, make sure, and rushing into the church with Lindsay of Dunrod, finished off the unfortunate Sir John Comyn. It was this incident which forced Bruce to seize the throne much sooner than he would have chosen. He knew that slaying a man before an altar would result in his excommunication – and no excommunicated individual could possibly be anointed king. He reckoned that it would take three weeks for the news to reach the Pope in Rome and another three for the sentence of excommunication to get back to Scotland. So he had only six weeks to mount the throne and hold his coronation, before the Scots bishops would receive papal orders forbidding their necessary part in the ceremony.

The Kirkpatrick family have retained the motto of "Mak Siccar" or "I Make Sure", ever since. A baronetcy was conferred on Thomas Kirkpatrick of Closeburn in 1685, a close adherent of the royal Stewarts, and the family and title still flourish – although not at Closeburn.

Robert Burns was a frequent visitor at the castle, where lived his friend Willie Stewart, factor of the estate and father of "Lovely Polly": this was when the Kirkpatricks and their successors had moved to the more modern mansion nearby. The old fortalice features in Walter Scott's *Old Mortality*.

The small town of Cumnock, in inland and upland Ayrshire, has a strange connection with the Bruce story, unflattering to either side in that epic struggle. In 1303, while he was still paying lip-service to Edward the First, who was in occupation of almost all Scotland, Bruce was appointed Sheriff of Lanark and Keeper of Ayr Castle by the English monarch, and we read that he was ordered to call up one thousand footmen from the Cumnock, Kyle and Cunninghame areas, which were outside his own earldom of Carrick, as well as another thousand from the earldom and his lands in Galloway – some indication of the populous state of these districts then. This force he was to send to Sir John de Botetourt, King Edward's bastard son, then Warden of the West March, to help in a major assault upon Wallace, Comyn and Sir Simon Fraser, then holding out in the wilds of Ettrick Forest. Undoubtedly Bruce "dragged his feet" in this effort, as he did in others of Edward's orders, and the force failed to capture the "rebels" in the Forest. Nevertheless, it was scarcely a creditable interlude in Bruce's career.

Then, four years later, in July 1307, Edward died at Lanercost near Carlisle, while on the point of once again invading Scotland. This was the occasion when, recognising that death was near, he had himself carried in a litter to the Solway Firth shore where he could look across to the Scots hills, and there cursed the country, Bruce, and its people; he then ordered that when he had drawn his last breath, his body should be boiled to dissolve all flesh from the bones. These last were to be carried on into Scotland, by his son the Prince of Wales, with the army, not being buried until that unruly kingdom was fully laid low once and for all, and Prince Edward was made to swear before all to perform this extraordinary last testament. This the son did, however reluctantly; but when his father expired, he (now Edward the Second) disobeyed and sent the body promptly back for suitable burial at Westminster. He then marched north with the great army. And it was Cumnock that he reached before this not very enthusiastic warrior decided that he had had enough of campaigning. He left Aymer de Valence, Earl of Pembroke, in charge of Scotland, and himself returned to London, not to return to the northern kingdom for three years.

So Cumnock hardly figures gloriously in the annals of this period. Nor indeed later when, during the religious troubles of 1685, the town was the scene of execution of sundry Covenanters. A year afterwards, the ashes of Alexander Peden, the famous preacher, buried in Auchinleck churchyard, were dug up by government dragoons and reinterred at the foot of Cumnock's gallows. The town used to be famous for the manufacture of snuff-boxes.

CUMNOCK Strathclyde
OS 71 NS 570200
Cumnock lies on the Lugar Water twenty miles south-east of Kilmarnock and seventeen miles east of Ayr, where the A70 and A76 meet.

Although a scarcely identifiable spot, with only the natural features of river, ravine and hillside to be seen, Dalrigh is an important name in Scotland's story. The word means "the meadow of the king", but it almost certainly refers to a king much earlier than Robert the Bruce. Somewhere here, in 1306, the newly-crowned Bruce suffered one of his most dire and dangerous setbacks and humiliations – and not at the hands of the pursuing English but those of the MacDougalls of Lorn, his own subjects.

Fleeing westwards for the safety of the Highland fastnesses after the disaster of Methven, on June the 19th, he and his wife, daughter, brothers and close friends, were ambushed in this narrow valley by Lame John MacDougall of Lorn, chief's son of that clan, who was a cousin of the murdered Red Comyn. The exact spot is hard to place today, although allegedly it was close to a tiny pond known as Lochan nan Arm, "the pool of the weapons". But then it was a running fight, up the valley, no real battle but a confused flight, for the King's party was surprised, and greatly outnumbered and burdened with the women, the child and the wounded. Many fell here, and how close Bruce himself came to capture or death can be gauged by the fact that his cloak was torn from him, and the clasp which had pinned it to his shoulder has remained a trophy with the MacDougall chiefs to this day, known as the Brooch of Lorn.

But escape the king did, with his women-folk and at least some of his friends.

DALRIGH Central
OS 50 NN 335296.
The site of the battle is not marked as such, but it is suggested that it took place about two miles east of Tyndrum, where the A82(T) threads the Pass of Strathfillan. St Fillan's chapel is at NN358284.

Recognising how impossible it was to continue thus in hostile country, he decided on sending his queen and daughter, in his brother Nigel's care, northwards to try eventually to reach Orkney, whilst he and his closest lieutenants headed into the lonely mountain wilderness, to start their long and dangerous wanderings. The sad parting would have been sadder still had they known that the Queen's party was to be betrayed, the Lord Nigel to be hanged and the women to be imprisoned in most shameful conditions. It was eight years before Bruce saw his wife and daughter again, after the victory of Bannockburn.

DALSWINTON Dumfries and Galloway
OS 78 NY 937854

Dalswinton is in Nithsdale, about nine miles north of Dumfries: it can be reached by a mile-long side road turning south-east off the A76(T) Dumfries-Sanquhar road, seven and a half miles north of Dumfries.

At Bruce's period, the Dalswinton area belonged to the Comyn family, who had a castle there, and it was frequently involved in the fighting during the Red Comyn's time of hostility to the English invaders. In 1301, when King Edward sent his son, the Prince of Wales, to initiate him into the business of subduing Scotland, the Scots used Comyn's Dalswinton as a base. From here they attacked the flanks of the Prince's host, not strong enough for any full-scale assault but harassing the enemy sufficiently much to depress Edward's not very militarily-inclined heir.

In 1306 the English chronicler Walter of Guisborough wrote a story about Dalswinton. He said that Bruce sent two of his brothers there from Lochmaben, his own castle – which itself is a mistake, for only Edward Bruce remained alive of the brothers at this time – to persuade the Red Comyn to come to the Greyfriars monastery at Dumfries, there to discuss their differences. We know what happened at Dumfries, when Bruce stabbed Comyn before the altar, with such dramatic consequences for Scotland; but whether this tale of coaxing John Comyn from Dalswinton to Dumfries is true, is very doubtful. Comyn was in fact in the county town, sitting as one of King Edward's justices at this time; and the generally accepted account of how Bruce learned of this, from a courier he waylaid en route to King Edward in London, is very different. Another English chronicler embroiders the story by adding that the the brothers were indeed sent by Bruce to assassinate Comyn at Dalswinton, but failed to do so because they found him so friendly! It must be remembered that after Bruce's taking of the throne, subsequent to Comyn's death, the English authorities were much concerned to destroy Bruce's good name and fame, especially at the Vatican.

After Comyn's death Bruce siezed Dalswinton Castle, along with other Comyn strongholds. But later, when the new-crowned king was a fugitive in the Highland West, the English re-captured them, and still held Dalswinton as late as 1313.

After Bruce's final triumph, the Dalswinton property was given to his faithful friends and supporters, Walter the High Steward (his son-in-law) and Sir Robert Boyd of Noddsdale.

The castle of Dalswinton is no more, with an eighteenth century mansion erected on the site, one mile south-east of the village, near the Nith's bank. It was the builder of this house, Patrick Miller, one of the agricultural improvers, who introduced the iron plough into Scotland; also the turnip. He also built and launched one of the earliest steamboats, on Dalswinton Loch, in 1788.

DOUGLAS Strathclyde
OS 71 NS 842318

Douglas is ten miles south-west of Lanark, via the A70: the map reference is to the castle.

The very name of this town conjures up mind-pictures of derring-do, heroism, bloodshed and war; also of course, shame, for the Douglases were not always heroes. A little burgh not particularly attractive in appearance today, it lies in the former coal-mining valley of the Douglas Water, or Douglasdale, in mid-Lanarkshire.

The two features of relevance to the Bruce period here are St Bride's Kirk and the site of the old Douglas Castle, which has twice been replaced, first by an early seventeenth century fortalice (of which only part of a round tower remains) and then by the castellated mansion of 1759, designed by Adam for the then Duke of Douglas.

Only the choir of the original church of St Bride's, with its crypt beneath, remains, somewhat altered, with a small spire. This was a thirteenth century foundation, a prebend of Glasgow Cathedral and the traditional burial-place of the Lords of Douglas. There is no sure record of when the Douglases first came here, or whether they gave their name to the area, or vice versa – *dubh glas* merely means

the dark stream, in Gaelic. The probability is that they were of early Celtic origin, rather than Norman. At any rate, a William Douglas who died in 1199 possessed Douglasdale, and his great-grandson was Sir William, known as Le Hardi, or "The Strong", whose eldest son was Bruce's friend and the greatest of his lieutenants – the famous Good Sir James, "the Black Douglas", so feared by the English that mothers used to hush their children to sleep with the words

'Hush ye, hush ye, do not fret ye
The Black Douglas will not get ye.'

His exploits, of course, would fill volumes. He it was whom Bruce charged on his death-bed at Cardross, with the task of removing his heart from his lifeless body and taking it on crusade. The king had vowed that he would lead a crusade to the Holy Land, against the Infidel, if God would but give him the kingdom, a vow which he had never been able to fulfil. Douglas obeyed his friend's last royal command and got as far as Spain with the heart. There he was asked by King Alfonso to assist in an attack on the Moors then occupying much of his kingdom. Douglas agreed, and at Tebay de Ardales, in 1330, the Scots found themselves alone and cut off. Leading a gallant charge against the Infidel, Sir James threw the royal heart in its silver casket ahead of him into the thick of the Moorish front shouting "Lead on brave heart, as thou wast ever wont to do! Douglas will follow." He did just that, and reaching the casket fell lifeless beside it, under a hail of blows. Other Scots knights died with him, but some escaped to bring home Douglas's body and Bruce's heart. The latter was buried in Melrose Abbey and the former in St Bride's Kirk. Ever since, the Douglas coat-of-arms has borne a red heart beneath the three silver stars on blue.

There were many other Douglas tombs in the Kirk and its crypt, although some have disappeared, for the church has been much reduced in size. Moreover it has been despoiled down the centuries, Cromwell's troops being blamed for much of the mutilation when, as so often, they stabled their horses in this building. There was also a major reconstruction in the nineteenth century.

The site of all three Douglas castles is less than a mile north-north-east of the town, down in the haughland of the river. Bruce himself came to the original fortalice early in his career, when Edward of England ordered him to go and arrest the wife and children of Sir William Douglas, who had been governor of Berwick Castle and had held out bravely against the English. Bruce's decision not to do this, and his merely mock attack on Douglasdale, led directly to his joining Wallace, the High Steward and other Scots leaders in the fight for independence, in which he had hitherto taken no part; as well as providing his first meeting with young James Douglas, Sir William's son.

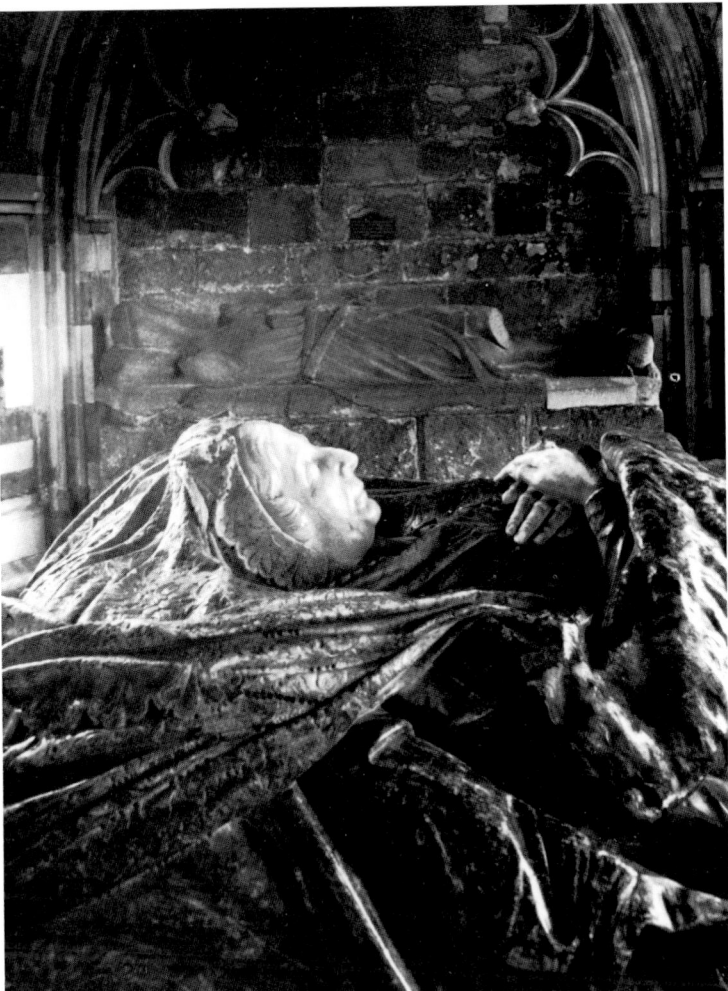

The most colourful story connected with this castle is, of course, that known as "The Douglas Larder". In 1307 the English held Douglas Castle, like so many another, and Sir James decided that this indignity must end and the castle be destroyed – since he could by no means hold it against the overwhelming English might. He sent a message to the enemy keeper thereof, one Sir John de Walton, declaring that he would repossess his house by Palm Sunday that year. When that day dawned and there had been no assault, Walton and most of his garrison went piously to church at St Bride's. But after the service Douglas appeared with a band of men and attacked the English, and in the fight killed Walton and twenty-six of his men, taking the remaining dozen prisoner. With the dead and wounded he made for the castle, where the porters and cooks had prepared a fine dinner for the church-goers. Sir James overpowered these without difficulty: and after collecting all that he wanted in arms, valuables and family heirlooms, he slaughtered his own cattle and stock; piled the meat inside with

Opposite, the ruins of St Brides Kirk. Above, beyond the relatively modern effigy of Lady Lucy Elizabeth Douglas may be seen the tomb of the Good Sir James of Douglas who, in 1330, was killed by the Moors while carrying the heart of Bruce through Spain to the Holy Land.

all the grain, meal and supplies held there by the enemy; put all in the hall where the banquet had been prepared, with the dead English and the bound prisoners on top; and set all alight, before marching off to rejoin Bruce. It was a grim vengeance – but such as the invaders were themselves perpetrating *ad nauseum* on Scotland.

Douglas Castle was the prototype of *Castle Dangerous* in Walter Scott's last romance.

In 1688 the 26th Regiment of foot, known as the Cameronians, was raised here under the command of the son of the second Marquis of Douglas.

The Good Sir James's nephew was raised to the dignity of Earl of Douglas; and as the generations passed, the power of this family rose to heights which rivalled and even exceeded at times that of the Crown, its members frequently intermarrying with the royal family.

The remains of the early seventeenth century tower on the site of the old castle at Douglas.

DUMFRIES Dumfries and Galloway
OS 84 NX 970760
Dumfries is eighty-two miles south of Glasgow, via the A74(T) and A701(T): and thirty-five miles north-west of Carlisle, via the A74(T) and A75(T).

The merest glance at the map will show why the ancient town of Dumfries inevitably had to become a prize to be fought over in any warfare between England and Scotland — and there was a sufficiency of that. For it sits above the River Nith only some seven miles inland from the Solway Firth, the south shores of which are English. So this, the largest and finest town of a great and productive area, known indeed as The Queen of the South, was only a few miles by sea from the English coast, with all that implied in invasion and counter-invasion.

In the Wars of Independence, therefore, Dumfries played a prominent part, and changed hands frequently. Even before those wars started, it was drawn into controversy, for in 1286 Bruce's grandfather, the Competitor, fifth Lord of Annandale, marched against it and took over town and castle by armed strength, (this within a month or two of Alexander the Third's accidental death over the Kinghorn cliff) to assert his claim to be next heir to the throne after the Infant Maid of Norway – who of course died shortly afterwards. John Balliol, Devorgilla of Galloway's son, was meantime making the same assertions; and these two were bound to clash. Dumfries was a rich bone for them to fight over.

In 1300 Edward of England himself came and took Dumfries, on his way to the siege of Caerlaverock Castle nearby; and it remained in English hands during the early part of the Wars of Independence period. Indeed, English justices were sitting in assize in its castle in 1306 when Bruce himself arrived here, after his hurried flight from England to escape the results of the Red Comyn's treachery – and found Comyn himself in the Greyfriars chapel and slew him before the

high altar, in an act of impulse which was to change the course of history.

The same year Edward Plantagenet had hanged Bruce's brother-in-law and friend, Sir Christopher Seton, here at Dumfries, on what was called the Crystal Mount; and later, on this eminence, Sir Christopher's widow, the Lady Christian Bruce, erected her chapel of the Holy Rood to her late husband's memory. This chapel is no more, but its site is occupied by the present St Mary's church at the north end of English Street.

Dumfries Castle is also gone. Greyfriars church, the more modern one, stands on its site fronting the north end of High Street. The position of the original Greyfriars chapel where Bruce slew Comyn is marked by a

plaque on a building in Castle Street, near the Friars Vennel.

It is perhaps sad that all these historic places are no more – but it is a long, long, time since the thirteenth and fourteenth centuries, and Dumfries has suffered grievous spoliation and fire in the interim, being comprehensively burned by the English in 1448 and again in 1536, as well as undergoing many lesser attacks.

There is still one feature, however, which has survived from that grim period, the Old Bridge over the Nith built by Devorgilla, heiress of the ancient Celtic Lords of Galloway. This fine edifice, now of only six arches but originally longer, has remained despite wars, floods and the demands of modern traffic, because it was built only for pedestrians, crossable only after mounting a flight of steps.

The graveyard of St Michael's church is also ancient, even though the church itself is less so, eight centuries of the Dumfries dead lying at peace therein: so this too was in use at Bruce's time. Robert Burns, who came to Dumfries in 1787, is buried there, with his wife and children.

Not far to the south-south-east, at Castledykes, is the site of the Comyn's castle, at a bend in the River Nith.

So this ancient red-stone town, full of character and tradition, is eminently worth visiting for anyone with the least interest in Robert the Bruce or indeed in almost any aspect of Scotland's colourful story.

Both abandoned at Dunaverty, the lifeboat launching ramp and the dramatic site of the castle which still retains some scanty stonework on its summit. Access to the site is by the golf course.

DUNAVERTY CASTLE
Strathclyde
OS 68 NR 687075.
Dunaverty Castle is at the southernmost tip of the Mull of Kintyre, ten miles south of Campbeltown by the B842 and a minor road through Southend

To penetrate right down to the tip of the forty-five mile long peninsula of Kintyre, in Argyll, from Tarbert, demands decision, for it is on the road to nowhere else; but it is worth the effort, the Mull of Kintyre being a highly dramatic place, scenically as well as geographically and indeed strategically. Here you are as far south as Alnwick in Northumberland, jutting like a clenched fist into the wild seas where the Atlantic joins the North Channel of the Irish Sea, a mere ten miles from the Antrim coast. The Mull's savage headland cliffs are a sight to behold, their lighthouse surely one of the most inaccessible spots in the British Isles, and the dizzy road thereto is not for the faint-hearted.

Less daunting to reach but still spectacular is Dunaverty Castle, crowning its rock-stack on a lesser headland half a mile south of the aptly-named Southend village, where all roads end. Here Dunaverty is a notable landmark, thrusting its challenge to the ocean, the fragmentary ruins of what was one of the most important castles of the great Lordship of the Isles, built on the site of a Pictish fort. Bruce gained Dunaverty during the six hectic

weeks between his murder of the Red Comyn and his coronation, just how is uncertain. But he was to be thankful that it was in good hands, those of his friend Angus Og of the Isles, soon thereafter. For here he came for refuge some months later, as a fugitive, after the defeats of Methven and Dalrigh, before he fled still further into the Hebrides.

Dunaverty may have provided a secure sanctuary temporarily, but it must have been an uncomfortable one, perched on its harsh rock above the turbulent seas which ever pound the Mull of Kintyre. The place has an air of savagery about it still, and savage has been its story down the years. James the Fourth besieged it two centuries later, in his campaign to bring down the Isles lordship; and almost before his royal fleet was out of sight thereafter, it was retaken by John of Islay and the King's keeper hanged from its walls. And in the Civil Wars period, Montrose's fiery lieutenant, Colkitto MacDonald, lost it to the Covenanting General Alexander Leslie, who thereafter massacred all 300 surrendered defenders, at the behest of the Covenant divines. The castle was then reduced to ruin.

Stone letters on the abbey tower proclaim that the hero king's body is buried within.

Dunfermline is, of course, a must for anyone concerned with following the steps of Robert Bruce, for here those steps often led him, in humiliation and in triumph – as here they were finally ended. The fact is proclaimed to all comers, for, high above the rest of the town, the abbey's tower spells out his name in great stone letters, as its balustrade.

The ancient town could not be more royal; for its abbey is sometimes called the Westminster of Scotland, and its place was a seat of the early Celtic monarchy long before Bruce's day. It stands on rising ground in West Fife, and there can be no difficulty in finding abbey and palace, for they are close together, and the tower of the former dominates the huddled town.

Start with the abbey, for it was there first, the original seat of Malcolm Canmore and the Celtic kings having been a fairly modest stone tower a little way to the west, in what is now Pittencrieff Park, and it would be there that Malcom brought his half-Saxon, half-Hungarian Margaret Atheling in 1069, to make her his queen. She herself soon afterwards built the great abbey, the first shrine of

the Roman Church to be erected in Scotland. She was to become the famous Saint Margaret, who had such a major impact on her adopted country's story. In her abbey she was buried, her difficult husband's body was brought to lie beside hers, and thereafter her sons, and all the Scots monarchs including Bruce himself. Previously the Kings of Scots had been buried on the sacred Hebridean isle of Iona, but Roman Catholic Margaret changed all that. She also got started on building the new palace, more suitably palatial than the old stark tower. The ruins thereof stand just to the west and south, all but linked to the abbey.

Bruce's first recorded visit here was anything but auspicious: indeed, it was one of the least glorious interludes of his career – for he was not always the hero-king. In the winter of 1303–4, Edward the First, after a savage and victorious progress through Scotland, made Dunfermline his headquarters; and there he summoned Bruce and the other "rebellious lords", with the country prostrate and all but cowed. Most came, including the Bruce, then aged twenty-nine: the Scottish

39

position was seemingly hopeless, he was unable to work with the hated John Comyn, and Wallace's star was in decline. And at Dunfermline Bruce was consistently and publicly humiliated by Edward and indeed sent, with a group of the toughest English commanders, to try to capture Wallace and Comyn and others hiding in the Ettrick Forest. That objective was not achieved, to Bruce's relief, but the humiliation remained. It is typical of Edward Longshanks that when, in the spring of 1304, he left Dunfermline, he burned the palace and tried to burn the abbey behind him.

In happier times Bruce built up both again, and came here frequently. And when, in 1327, Elizabeth de Burgh, his queen, died, sorrowing he buried her in the abbey amongst the other royal tombs. On his own death-bed at Cardross, in 1329, he gave his friend, Sir James Douglas, his strict instructions: his rib-cage was to be opened on death, and his heart extracted and taken on the long-promised crusade against the Infidel, but the rest of his body was to be buried in Dunfermline Abbey alongside Elizabeth's. This was duly done.

There is a sequel. In 1818, when the east end of the abbey was being rebuilt to form the present large parish church of the town, excavations unearthed the king's body. There was no doubt but that it was Bruce's because of the sawn-open rib-cage. The skeleton was wrapped in a pall of cloth-of-gold covering two layers of sheet-lead, all within a stone coffin. Reverently the remains were reinterred before the pulpit of the new church, under a handsome brass memorial plate, where all who visit may pay their respects. Nearby, in recent years, fine stained glass windows pay their colourful tribute. Indeed the entire later church at the east end of the abbey is almost a mausoleum to the man who transformed himself from a somewhat irresponsible playboy into the saviour of his country. The aforementioned tower, 103 feet high, declares its message loud and clear.

There is not a great deal left of the palace, but sufficient to show that it has been a very fine and ornate building, added to of course down the centuries. James the First of Scots was born herein, as was the ill-fated Charles the First.

The great hall of the royal palace with its semi-subterranean cellars and storerooms revealed.

Dunollie stands high and proud on its rock above the Firth of Lorn a bare mile north of Oban, a typical stronghold of a Highland chief, in this case MacDougall of MacDougall. It is now ruinous but still impressive. Its later successor, the present seat of the clan chief, is nearby. The castle, private property, is plainly visible from the shore or from the water, a landmark much exclaimed over by passengers on the Oban-Mull ferry.

As far as Bruce was concerned, this was enemy territory, for its lairds in his time were Alexander MacDougall, Lord of Argyll, and his son Ian Bacach, or Lame John of Lorn, one of the King's most determined opponents. Descended from Dougal, eldest son of the great Somerled, first Lord of the Isles, Alexander of Argyll had married a Comyn, and was indeed uncle of the murdered Red Comyn. He became a supporter of John Balliol, therefore, and remained loyal to that sorry monarch, and so inimical to Bruce. His son, Lame John, half a Comyn, was probably the hero-king's most bitter enemy in all Scotland.

It was John Macdougall's men who ambushed the royal party as they fled through Strathfillan after the disastrous Battle of Methven in 1306, where took place the incident of one of them snatching at Bruce and managing to tear off his cloak with its fine shoulder-brooch. That jewel, known ever after as the Brooch of Lorn, became the proudest possession of the MacDougalls, and still remains at Dunollie.

After the Bruce victory at the Pass of Brander, Lame John's activities were much circumscribed, but he could still write to Edward of England, who made him his Admiral of the Western Seas, assuring him of his devotion and promising all possible support. He indeed did remain a thorn in Bruce's flesh, and led a naval expedition against the king in 1311.

On Bruce's eventual triumph, and when he felt strong enough to enforce it, Lame John's lands were forfeited and Dunollie was granted to Sir Arthur Campbell, kin to Sir Neil of Lochawe, the King's close friend and noted lieutenant. But the MacDougalls got it back in due course, when John's son Ewan married an illegitimate grand-daughter of the king. And it has remained with them ever since, despite their support for the Stewart cause in Jacobite times.

Walter Scott wrote about Dunollie. And William Wordsworth, when he visited here in 1831, was shocked to find a live eagle kept in chains within the ruin.

DUNOLLIE CASTLE
Strathclyde
OS 49 NM 852316
Dunollie Castle is on the northern outskirts of Oban, just off the A85 by a side road: it can be easily seen from the seashore road to Ganavan.

A tranquil scene from Dunollie across the Sound of Kerrera.

DUNSTAFFNAGE CASTLE
Strathclyde
OS 49 NM 882345

Dunstaffnage Castle is five miles north of Oban, via the main A85 and a side road: it can, however, easily be seen from the A85.

This great and finely preserved fortress-castle has inevitably a similar history to that of Dunollie, from which it is distant only three miles: at least as far as the Bruce period is concerned, it being the main seat of Alexander MacDougall, Lord of Argyll, whilst Dunollie was that of his son, Lame John MacDougall of Lorn. So much that applies to the one does so also to the other.

Crowning a low rocky knoll at the tip of a promontory projecting into the mouth of Loch Etive from the Firth of Lorn, it is now open to the public. It consists of a massive quadrangular curtain-walled castle, with masonry up to eleven feet thick, and round towers at three angles, plus a gatehouse-tower at the fourth, wherein is the entrance, fifteen feet above ground, now reached by a stone forestair but formerly only by a removable bridge. There is a courtyard of uneven level within, corresponding to the top of the rock-formation, and a late sixteenth century tower-house has been built herein, soaring above even the sixty-foot walling. There are also eighteenth century additions.

Dunstaffnage was an important place from early times, a seat of government of the Dalriadic Scots kingdom before its amalgamation with the Pictish realm of Alba. Here the Stone of Destiny was brought, from Iona and Dunadd, for safety from the Vikings, before it was taken to Scone. The castle featured in the stirring times of Somerled the Mighty, first Lord of the Isles, and became the seat of the descendants of his eldest son Dougal, the Lords of Argyll.

So, with Alexander MacDougall of Argyll marrying a Comyn, and being uncle of the Red Comyn whom Bruce slew at Dumfries, this stronghold came firmly into the opposition camp against the hero-king, along with Dunollie. After the Pass of Brander victory, in 1308, Bruce besieged it:

The top photograph on this page shows a monumental fireplace which brings a sense of domesticity to the stark castle ruin. Right, modern concrete supporting lintels contrast with the roughly coursed rubble walls of a formidable tower.

'That stoute wes, stark and bauld,
    Till Dunstaffnych rycht sturdely
A sege set.'

The place had to yield, however, and the king thereafter made it a royal fortress. But he granted a charter to Sir Archibald Campbell, as hereditary Constable or Keeper, an honour still held by a Campbell, as Captain of Dunstaffnage.

Since then the castle has seen much incident. David the Second, Bruce's rather ineffective son, dated a charter from here in 1355. And here the last Earl of Douglas fled after James the Second murdered his brother, to try to persuade the then Lord of the Isles to make retaliatory war on the King. James the Fourth twice came to Dunstaffnage. And in 1715 and 1745 government troops were quartered in the castle to counter the Jacobites. Flora MacDonald was for a short time a prisoner here in 1746.

Against the picturesque background of the West Highland and Hebridean seaboard, Dunstaffnage is a place to be visited.

The castle was built to exactly fit its rocky setting. The upper works of the seventeenth century insertion are evident. Left, plaster-facing once covered all the interior walls of the castle as on the wall seen here.

43

ETTRICK FOREST Borders
OS 73

The heart of Ettrick Forest is the area bounded to the north by the A72 from Peebles to Selkirk, and to the east and south by the A7(T) from Selkirk to Hawick and Langholm. Ordnance Survey sheet 73 covers much of this area.

This name is misleading today, giving the impression that it applies only to the valley of the River Ettrick, in the central Borderland, and its vicinity. Whereas it used to be the term given to an infinitely vaster area, indeed to most of the Middle March, from Jedburgh on the east to Langholm on the west, from Peebles and Biggar almost to Lanark on the north, the extensive womb of waters wherein rise the great rivers of Tweed and Clyde, Teviot and Annan and many another, besides Ettrick and Yarrow. Selkirk, or Shiel Kirk, the church-place of the high summer pastures, was its accepted "capital". When the simpler name, "The Forest", was spoken of in Lowland Scotland, it was referring to this huge slice of upland territory, over 400 square miles.

It was not all forest, of course, in the sense of being covered with trees, although undoubtedly there would be much more scrub woodland than there is today. The word was used in the same sense as a Highland deer-forest is termed still, where indeed there may be no trees at all. It formed, in Bruce's day and for long after, a sort of redoubt, a natural fortress-area, almost impenetrable by large forces, unconquerable. So its mountains and rivers and lochs, its bogs and thickets and passes, were always a haunt of broken men and fugitives, and robbers too – and the Borderland was always apt to have a notable supply of these.

Thus it was, needless to say, of outstanding importance to men fighting against overwhelming odds to free Scotland of its invaders, a refuge and gathering-place, often the only sanctuary left to them. Wallace and Bruce had to use it extensively throughout the long years of struggle; indeed it was here that Wallace was proclaimed Guardian of the Realm in March 1298.

So the part played by the Forest of Ettrick can hardly be overestimated, especially in the earlier period. Today we tend not to see it as an entity in itself, but as many individual areas of the lovely land of the central Borders – Tweeddale and Tweedsmuir, Teviotdale, Upper Clydesdale, Megget, Ettrick and Yarrow and the rest; but it would be a pity not to grasp the significance of the combination of all these, of the area as a whole, not only during the Wars of Independence but in the centuries to follow. Highly important meetings, as well as armed assaults, musterings and groupings were staged herein: for instance at Stobo, near Peebles, in the upper Tweed valley, where William Lamberton, Bishop of St Andrews had a remote manor; and at Biggar, where the Battle of Roslin was planned.
See **Selkirk, Stobo.**

The extensive upland country of Ettrick Forest, once the haunt of robbers and hunted Scots patriots.

Falkirk is eleven miles south of Stirling by the A9, and just over twenty-five miles west-north-west of Edinburgh, via the M9. The battlefield is to the south-east of the town, south of the A803.

The body of the Scottish hero Sir John de Graham was brought to this tomb in the parish churchyard from the nearby battlefield.

The busy industrial town of Falkirk in south Stirlingshire might not seem to have much to do with Robert Bruce and his period; and admittedly there is only one surviving man-made feature here relating to those days. But the topography and outline of the land does not change greatly, and the strategic import-ance of Falkirk and district can be perceived by anyone with an eye for country, aided by a glance at the map.

Stirling, of course, was the cockpit of Scot-land, for here was the first possible crossing of Forth, save by boat, at the very waist of the land. So all traffic between North and South Scotland, as between Highlands and Low-lands, had to funnel through Stirling. And Falkirk, only eleven miles to the south, was

the gateway from south and east. Not only so, but two natural features channelled all traffic through Falkirk. Between the town and the narrowing Forth, to the east, lay un-drained carseland and marshy flats, through which meandered the muddy River Carron; and, still more important, to west and north extended the vast hilly wilderness of the Tor Wood, the largest area of forest in the Low-lands after that of Ettrick – hard to visualise now when most of the woods have gone and industry has risen in their stead. But then, and for long after, a daunting barrier stretched all the way to Stirling itself, some fifty square miles, all but trackless save for the road the Romans had built between the two centres.

With some recognition of all this, it will be

seen how vital Falkirk was in any struggle for Scotland. The Romans had recognised this well, and built their Antonine Wall to help cope with this strategic situation, and their road northwards at its end.

William Wallace's name, of course, is more often connected with Falkirk than is Bruce's, for here it was, in 1298, only a few miles from his great victory at Stirling Bridge the year before, that he suffered major defeat at the hands of King Edward and his vastly superior army – largely on account of the desertion on the field of many of the Scots nobles, who resented this "upstart patriot". There are differences of opinion as to whether Bruce himself was present at the Battle of Falkirk. One school of thought claims that he was at that time on the other side of Scotland, in his own territory of Ayrshire, attacking English-held Ayr Castle and burning it. This he certainly did towards the end of August that year; but Falkirk was fought a month earlier and this writer holds the opinion that Bruce came through from the west, arriving late on the scene, but was in time to take part in the rescue of Wallace's person from the stricken field. There are indications of this, and it would account for much that followed.

The battle was fought in the foothills area about a mile south-east of the town, in the Callendar and Westquarter vicinities, south of the A803 approaches where the Westquarter Burn come down from Glen to what is now Callendar Park. A reasonably good tactical site for a defensive battle –

although Wallace did not want to face the English might, in heavy cavalry and archers, at this time, but was forced to it by circumstances. At least the great Tor Wood was there behind him, as an escape route for the survivors, however reluctant he was personally to leave the scene of disaster.

The following year Bruce was back at Falkirk, now as Joint Guardian with the Red Comyn, having trouble with that difficult character, and issuing governmental documents addressed from the Tor Wood. And in 1314, before the Battle of Bannockburn, he chose this area as the rendezvous for the assembly of the army which was to face and finally defeat the English might. Bruce did not intend to *fight* in the Falkirk vicinity, but to decoy the enemy northwards to the still wider and more boggy carselands where the Bannock Burn joined Forth. Nevertheless, this Falkirk-Tor Wood area played a vital part in the run-up to the great victory.

In the graveyard of the old parish church at Falkirk is the grave and renovated tombstone of the renowned Sir John de Graham, who fell at Wallace's side in the battle; also that of Sir John Stewart of Bonkyl.

"Here lyes Sir John the Grame, baith wight and wise,
" Ane of the chiefs who reschewit Scotland thrice;
Ane better knight not the world was lent, Nor was gude Grame of truth and hardiment."

FORFAR Tayside
OS 54 NO 460510
*Forfar is fourteen miles north of
Dundee, via the A929.*

As the seat of a royal castle, this ancient royal burgh, the county town of Angus, had its part to play in much of Scotland's early story. Malcolm Canmore is believed to have built the stronghold here, and his wife Margaret, queen and saint, had a retreat on an island in nearby Forfar Loch. The castle was erected on a mound at the north-east end of the town, still called Castlehill, its site marked now by an octagonal tower which once acted as the Market Cross.

In the Wars of Independence, William Wallace no doubt did not ignore Forfar, since he had strong connections with Dundee in the same county; but it came to prominence in 1291, under peculiar circumstances which shed an interesting light on the niceties of baronial, if not chivalric, behaviour in what was in so many ways a barbarous age. When Edward of England acted as arbiter to decide

on the claims to the Scots throne, following on the death of the Maid of Norway, he insisted on the resignation of the Guardians or Regents, and the handing over to him of all royal Scottish castles – and so anxious were the various competitors for the throne that they agreed to these humiliating terms. But, of all men who might have been expected to acquiesce happily, Gilbert de Umfraville, Earl of Angus in his mother's right and an Englishman, courteously refused to yield up Forfar Castle, on the grounds that its keeping had been entrusted to him, not by the King of England but by the Community of the Realm of Scotland; and only at their behest could he legitimately render it. And since the Guardians of that day had been forced to resign by Edward, there was nobody so to instruct him. However, with the Guardians in due course reappointed by

Edward, although now under his authority, the way was clear for this stickler for formalities to hand over the castle without bloodshed or loss of face. On this occasion Edward Plantagenet appears to have been unusually patient and condescending, no doubt because Umfraville was a powerful noble in England as well as in Scotland. An odd if scarcely glorious incident.

When next Forfar comes into prominence in the national struggle, the circumstances were very different. This was in 1308, two years after Bruce's coronation, when his struggle for the throne he had prematurely occupied was grim indeed. With the aid of one Philip, his surname not recorded but keeper of the royal forest of Plater nearby, the king attacked Forfar Castle secretly on the night of Christmas, when the English garrison were presumably celebrating the feast more well than wisely. Scaling the walls by means of ladders and ropes, the Scots managed to gain unopposed access, and proceeded to slaughter everyone therein. Therafter, in accordance with his policy of denying all such places to the invading forces, Bruce ordered the demolition of the castle. It was never rebuilt. Later, much of the stonework was used to build the Old Steeple and many a house of the town. It is fairly obvious that this feat of Bruce and the Forester of Plater could not have been achieved without some co-operation from the citizens of Forfar.

There used to be a track which ran eastwards from Forfar some seventeen miles to Ulysseshaven, or Usan as it is usually called, just south of Montrose; this is known as the King's Codger's Road, and along it fresh fish could be hurried for the royal table at Forfar Castle.

This miniature round tower set in its walled garden, marks the site of Forfar Castle. It is reached by a gated passage in Canmore Street, a turning off Castle Street opposite the stationer's shop from which the key may be borrowed. From the top of the tower, bearing its monogram of Charles I, the climber is treated to a panoramic view of the town.

*The fourteen-mile valley of Glen
Dochart runs south-westwards,
threaded by the river and the A85
highway, from the head of Loch Tay
at Killin to Crianlarich, where the A85
joins the A82 coming up Glen Falloch
from Loch Lomondside. The map
reference is to Loch Dochart castle.*

Glen Dochart is a pleasant open and green vale for most of the way, flanked by 3000-foot mountains, but closing in at the western end, under Ben More and Stobinian, wooded here and embosoming the twin lochs of Iubhair and Dochart, separated only by a quarter-of-a-mile of river. Motorists from the south-east to Oban and Fort William will know it well.

Here was the sanctuary of that famous eighth century Celtic saint and missionary, Fillan, of noble Irish birth, who was renowned for his ability to cure mental ailments and whose holy well Walter Scott has made celebrated:

> "St Fillan's blessed well,
>   Whose spring can frenzied
> dreams dispel
>   And the crazed brain restore . . ."

Fillan's reputation was great in old Scotland, and this whole area was the centre of his activities, to which pilgrims and sufferers came from far and near. The local names testify to this – Strathfillan, a sort of continuation north-westwards of Glen Dochart; St Fillans village at the foot of Loch Earn; and Killin itself, which is a corruption almost certainly of Kilfillan. His actual hermitage and chapel was in Strathfillan, three miles west of Crianlarich; but by Bruce's time Glen Dochart seems to have been the location favoured by his successors and the custodians of his relics. The centre of his worship was probably the wooded island in Loch Dochart, where are now to be seen the ruins of a castle; but this is of late sixteenth century date, post-Reformation, and the fortalice was almost certainly built on the site of the original monastic buildings.

The main representative of the saint was called the Dewar of the Coigreach. Dewars or deuchars were hereditary custodians of Celtic saints' relics, and were always provided with a "dewar's croft", or farm, to help sustain them; and this one seems to have been in Glen Dochart. The coigreach was the saint's pastoral staff or crook. But by Bruce's time local power was also exercised by the descendants of the Celtic Abbots of Glendochart, a hereditary line who "managed" St Fillan's shrine – a quite normal feature in the Columban Church. These descendants had become the Clan Macnab, that is Mac-an-Abb, the Sons of the Abbot.

When Bruce and his close companions, including his queen, fled westwards in 1306 after the defeat of Methven, they were succoured here by the Dewar of the Coigreach but opposed apparently by the chief of Macnab – at least this last is assumed, because when the king eventually came into his own, he ejected Patrick Macnab of Glendochart and gave the barony to Menzies of Weem. The Macnabs got it back of course, eventually – and an awkward and proud lot they seem to have been, ecclesiastical descent or none. Two little anecdotes will serve to illustrate this. Once, at a great gathering of chiefs and nobles, there was a mighty jockeying for precedence at a long table. Macnab, however, just sat down in no lofty position, observing that wherever Macnab sat *was* the head of the table. The other story refers to a question asked by an English governmental visitor of the 12th Macnab of Glendochart, in the mid eighteenth century, about the district's relations with lawful authority in the South. Macnab answered that "there was once a cratur callit exciseman sent up to my country – but they killt him."

Bruce's succour and blessing, in his hour of need, from the Dewar of the Coigreach was never forgotten; and on the eve of Bannockburn the King led a special veneration of the relics of St Fillan and invoked the saint's aid.

Pasture land does not change down the centuries, and below, the swirling waters of Killin Falls.

51

GLEN TROOL Dumfries and
Galloway
OS 77 NX 422798

*To reach this remote area, Glen Trool,
from Newton Stewart, follow the
A714 up the Cree valley northwards
for some ten miles, to Bargrennan,
where a right fork is taken which after
a couple of miles sends off on the
right another side-road, which leads
into and up Glen Trool. The reference
is to the battlefield.*

*Erected six centuries after his death,
this Bruce cairn marks the site of King
Robert's first major victory over the
English invaders.*

This attractive and remote valley of upland Galloway is important in the Bruce story, for it marks his first real victory in the field against a major English force, after his coronation, the disaster of Methven and his flight and wanderings in the West Highlands. In February 1307 he ventured a return, from the Isle of Arran, to his own earldom of Carrick, in Ayrshire. There, at his castle of Turnberry, he succeeded in defeating and ejecting the English garrison. But this was only a comparatively minor success, giving him a little time to find his feet, as it were, and gather a scratch force of supporters. However, King Edward sent Aymer de Valence, Earl of Pembroke, the victor of Methven, north again with a large army (including the Plantagenet's own illegitimate son Sir John de Botetourt, Henry Percy of Northumberland and John Mac-Dougall of Lorn) to put an end to the insolent "usurper" Bruce once and for all. Bruce took to the hills of south Ayrshire and north Galloway, where the heavily-armoured English cavalry and their archers would tend to be at a disadvantage, and in April he managed to ambush Pembroke and part of his army in the narrow glen.

The scene of this victory is at the east end, or head, of Loch Trool, the most beautiful loch in Galloway, lying some fifteen miles north of Newton Stewart, in the Galloway Forest Park. Here, below the steeps of Mulldonach, Bruce trapped the English cavalry on the marshy flats and broke up their formations by hurling rocks down upon them from the craggy mountainside.

He then forced the confused enemy into the soft ground where the horses got bogged down, and thereby divided Botetourt's and Percy's forces as well as scattering them – an early example of the genius Bruce developed for using the land to fight for him. A cairn-memorial, erected in 1929 (the sexcentenary of the hero-king's death) stands on high ground above the loch-head – not to be confused with the Covenanters' Memorial and Martyrs' Graves which are to be found at the other or west end of the loch.

The Falls of Buchan, near the Bruce Cairn, are another picturesque feature of a very lovely scene.

Romantically situated on the lip of a precipitous cliff above the River North Esk, in Midlothian, not very far from Roslin Castle on the other side of the valley, this fine castle is renowned as the birthplace of the poet William Drummond of Hawthornden, "the Scottish Petrarch" (1585–1649). But it has traditional links with both Bruce and Wallace, and highly dramatic links they are.

Oddly enough, the Bruce connection lies underneath the fifteenth and seventeenth century fortalice. For, reached by a ladder down a daunting well-shaft, is an intricate series of artificial caves carved out of the solid sandstone cliff and linked by long, dark passages, almost certainly of prehistoric construc-tion. These were allegedly used by the hero-king as a hiding-place and secret base during his struggle, at various times. Three of them are named the King's Gallery, the King's Diningroom and the King's Bedchamber; and one has its walling astonishingly carved into hundreds of stone nesting-boxes for pigeons, providing a source of food, the birds being able to fly out from an aperture in the cliff-face. Queen Victoria visited here in 1842. Nearby is a jut of rock overhanging the river, known as John Knox's Pulpit.

The castle itself is as picturesque as its setting, perched above the deep wooded valley. Permission to view must be obtained from the owners.

HAWTHORNDEN CASTLE
Lothian
OS 66 NT 286637
Hawthornden Castle, eight miles south-east of Edinburgh, is reached from the A6094 road, turning off to the west at Rosewell, five miles south-west of Dalkeith, and in half-a-mile reaching a private drive down to the castle, which is private property.

The Church's Part

It is not unimportant to recognise the quite large part played by Holy Church in the Wars of Independence, on both sides – though it was to the Bruce's very great advantage that, by and large, the prominent churchmen of Scotland were on his side. Bishop William Lamberton of St Andrews, the Primate, was one of his greatest and most useful supporters as well as his personal friend; Bishop Robert Wishart of Glasgow much encouraged Bruce and was one of the leaders in the fight against King Edward in the early days; Bishop William Fraser, Lamberton's predecessor at St Andrews, was prominent as one of the Guardians of the Realm; Master Nicholas Balmyle, later Bishop of Dunblane, was a loyal aide; Master Baldred Bisset helped also, and pleaded Scotland's cause usefully before the Vatican; and Bernard de Linton, Abbot of Arbroath and later Bishop of Sodor and Man, had been Bruce's secretary and in fact was the author of the famous Declaration of Independence, signed at his abbey of Arbroath in 1320 – on which, incidentally, some of the wording of the American Declaration of Independence is based. Other clerics were likewise to the fore in the struggle, including that warlike character Bishop William Sinclair of Dunkeld, whom Bruce was apt to refer to as "his own bishop" and who in 1316 personally seized a lance from a less militant knight and led the attack on English invaders of the Fife coast, gaining the victory. There were prelates who took a different view, to be sure, Comyn or Balliol supporters, notably Master William Comyn, Provost of the Chapel-Royal and a brother of the Earl of Buchan. But these were few.

Sweetheart Abbey was founded by Devorgilla in 1273. Her truncated effigy, which may be seen in the southeast transept of the ruined abbey church, still clutches the "sweet heart" of her husband John Balliol, to whose memory she dedicated the church.

The reason behind the Church's resistance to English domination and support for Bruce was essentially patriotic, and not only on the national or civil front. It stemmed from the pretensions and claims of the *English* Church. Because it so happened that there was no archbishop in Scotland at this stage, the Archbishops of York and Canterbury argued that, since all Christendom ought to be under the control of Metropolitans of archiepiscopal status, and there was none north of York, York must therefore have the spiritual hegemony over Scotland and the Scottish Church must be subservient to the English. Needless to say, this piece of ecclesiastical arrogance suited the Kings of England in their ambitions to be overlords of Scotland, and so Church and State worked together against the northern kingdom. Bishop Beck of Durham was one of Edward's chief *military* commanders – and one of the most savage; Master Hugh Cressingham, Vicar of Rudby, was made Treasurer of Scotland, but was killed leading the English army at Stirling Bridge; Master Walter of Amersham was made Chancellor or chief minister of Scotland; Master Ralph Manton, of the King's Wardrobe, was actually put in charge of Bruce himself, by Edward, but was slain at the Battle of Roslin – and so on. It was the Church Militant indeed, on both sides.

And it happened that Holy Church, in Scotland, was very rich. This was largely thanks to King David the First, son of Malcolm Canmore and Queen Margaret the Saint, who while a hostage in England had married one of the richest heiresses in that land and gained great wealth through her, with manors in no fewer than eleven English counties. His

reign coincided in the main with a peaceful interlude between the kingdoms – his sister was queen to Henry the First – and he, being like his mother of a religious frame of mind, was able to spend much of the vast Huntingdon revenues on building and staffing abbeys, priories and monasteries. It was not all piety, there being a sound practical reason behind it also. For David it was who devised and instituted the parish system in Scotland, in a great effort to limit the power over the people (and jurisdiction in local government), of the over-great nobles. So the country was divided up into parishes, each not only with a parish church but with local government responsibilities. But to staff all this huge number of parishes David required huge numbers of priests, educated incumbents. And to produce these the far-sighted monarch needed seminaries and schools – which was what the abbeys and priories were for. So Scotland in the twelfth century gained an extraordinary number of fine abbeys and religious houses, far more in proportion to the population than in England or probably elsewhere in Christendom – the ruins and relics of which are still one of the country's principal tourist attractions. Just think of Jedburgh, Kelso, Melrose and Dryburgh Abbeys, all within a few miles of each other. This went on all over the kingdom, outwith the Highlands. Thus, thanks to David, the Church was rich in land and buildings, in manpower and money, for it was vigorous in its encouragement of trade and manufacture and agriculture, and of course invaluable in its influence over the common people. A most valuable ally for the hero-king in his efforts to free his country.

A selection of the fine stone carving to be seen at Dryburgh Abbey, Borders.

HOLYROOD ABBEY Lothian
OS 66 NT 270739

*The remains of Holyrood Abbey are
incorporated in the grounds of
Holyroodhouse, which is at the foot of
the Canongate in Edinburgh: open to
the public.*

The Abbey of the Holy Rood, at Edinburgh, founded by David the First, is a sufficiently famous place in its own right, where much that was important in Scotland's history has taken place. It does not feature largely in Bruce's story, being usually in English hands throughout the Wars of Independence, as was Edinburgh itself, and did not represent any vital challenge in that struggle. But it did come into prominence in 1322, eight years after Bannockburn; when, in retaliation for a Scottish raid into England, Edward the Second ventured north again into Lothian with a large force, whilst the Scots main army was known to be north of Forth. He then sacked Holyrood abbey. However, their own depredations and Bruce's scorched-earth policy meant that the English invaders were not able to feed themselves off the country and they had to retire. It was reported that only a single cow was encountered in all Lothian, at Tranent, the Earl of Surrey remarking that it was the dearest beef that he had ever seen, and must have cost £1,000

and more! Sir James Douglas came hastening to attack the enemy flanks and rear, and the expedition faded away.

Bruce held Parliaments in the abbey in March 1327 and again a year later, this last in preparation for the much sought-after peace treaty with England. Edward the Third was now on the throne, and the abbey was to be the scene of this much happier occasion, marred for Scotland only by Bruce's growing physical weakness, so that he was in fact confined to a bedchamber in the monastic buildings. Here what is known as the Treaty of Northampton and Edinburgh was at last signed and sealed, the official English delegation being led by the Bishop of Lincoln, Lord High Treasurer; Sir Geoffrey le Scrope, Chief Justice; the Bishop of Norwich; and Bruce's old foe, Sir Henry Percy.

So Holyrood, if it came late into the picture, at least saw the triumphant conclusion of the struggle.

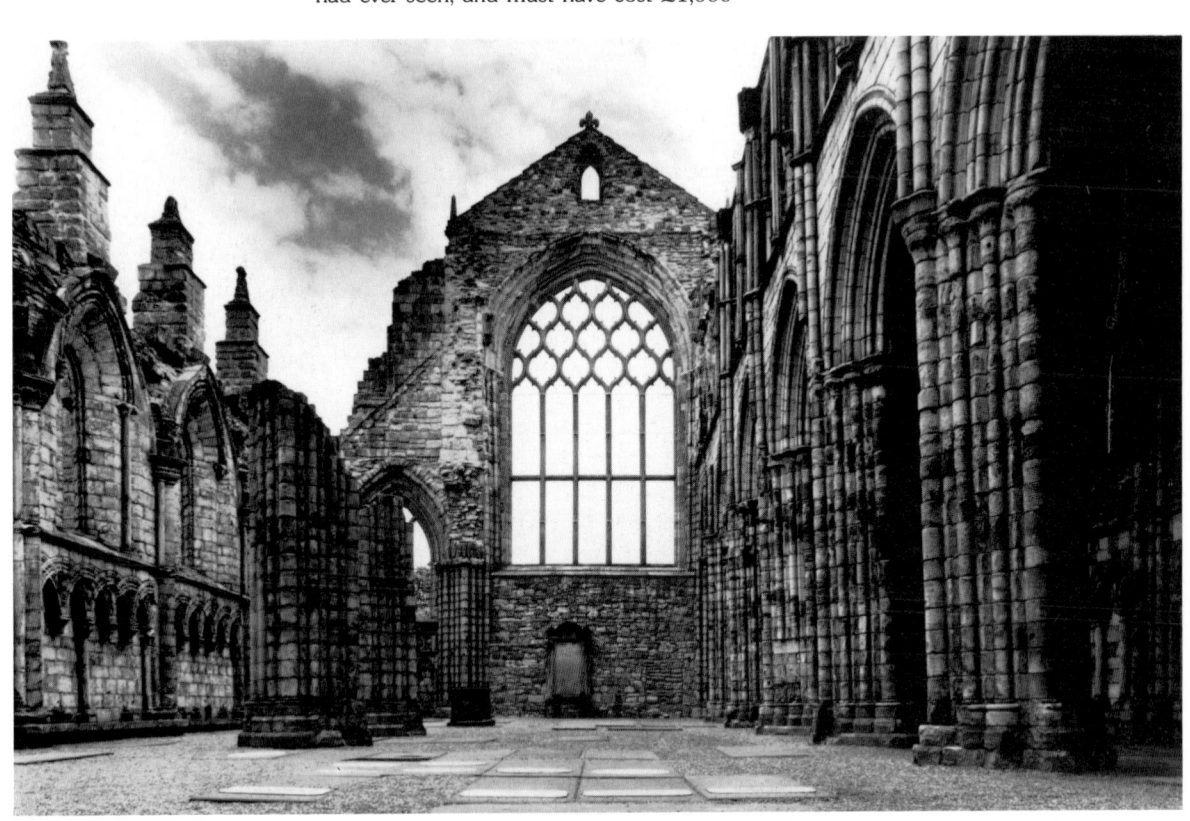

The great east window, and right, the richly decorated west door of Holyrood Abbey, so named because of the portion of Christ's true cross held by David I, Bruce's predecessor, which on this spot brought about a supposed miracle.

INCHAFFRAY ABBEY Tayside
OS 58 NO 954225
Inchaffray Abbey is situated in Strathearn, five miles west by south of Methven and about the same distance east of Crieff, lying a mile south of the main A85 highway, by a side-road striking off to Madderty.

This is probably one of the least-known abbeys in Scotland – and its ruins are now in a sad state. But it featured quite prominently in the Wars of Independence, for its abbot, Maurice, was a faithful and useful adherent of Robert Bruce. Its scanty remains stand on the level plain on the bank of the Pow Water, on what was once an island in marshland – hence the name of inch or island. A side-road was, in fact, driven right through the ruins of the abbey in 1816, a sorry act of vandalism, when stone coffins and an ivory cross were unearthed. Inchaffray was founded by Gilbert, third Earl of Strathearn, in 1200.

In 1299 Bruce and the Red Comyn, as Joint Guardians of the Realm, issued edicts from here, still in the name of the exiled King John Balliol. Abbot Maurice is believed to have taken part in Bruce's coronation at Scone, in 1306. Soon thereafter was the defeat at Methven, and almost certainly the King's fleeing party called in at the abbey on their way to the Highland West. The new monarch showed his gratitude for aid received by giving grants of the lands of Killin and Strathfillan to Inchaffray, these having hitherto held by the Macnabs, who did not support him. And interestingly, Christina of Mar and Garmoran, who befriended Bruce in his lonely Highland wanderings, followed the royal example by giving to Inchaffray Abbey the lands of Carinish in North Uist and the chapel of the Holy Trinity there – which cannot have been a very convenient outpost for a Strathearn monastery.

Once Bruce returned, to initiate his campaign for the recovery of his kingdom from English occupation, Abbot Maurice was ever helpful. In 1307 he assisted in the election of Nicholas Balmyle, Official of St Andrews and Bruce's Chancellor of the Realm, as Bishop of Dunblane. It is noteworthy that when Balmyle died in 1322, Abbot Maurice himself became Bishop of Dunblane. In 1313 he was given a safe-conduct to proceed through England to the court of Edward the Second, on a peace-mission – which was most evidently unsuccessful since the next year Edward invaded Scotland in great strength, in the campaign which was to end in his humiliating defeat at Bannockburn.

Undoubtedly the good Abbot of Inchaffray's most renowned activity was his barefoot blessing of Bruce's army before that great battle, when he carried before the army the precious arm-bone of St Fillan, whom the king looked upon as his personal protector.

INCHMAHOME Central
OS 57 NS 574005
Situated on an islet in the Lake of Menteith, which lies south of the A873, fifteen miles west of Stirling and four miles east of Aberfoyle. The priory ruins are now in the care of the Department of the Environment, and visitors are transported to the island by boat from the east end of the loch, a most worth-while excursion. Huge chestnut trees on the isle are reputed to have been grown from chestnuts brought from Rome.

The islet in the Lake of Menteith – properly the *Loch* of *Monteith*, of course, despite tales that it is the only lake in Scotland, the result of some English cartographer's ignorance in the 18th century – is best known as the safe refuge chosen for Mary Queen of Scots in 1547. At that time, Henry the Eighth of England was trying to seize the five year old princess as bride for his only son Edward and so to win Scotland, in what has become known as the Rough Wooing. But long before that it had Bruce connections.

The loch lies just south of the A873, below the very skirts of the Highland Line, in the midst of the low-lying Flanders Moss area. It is in fact a great widening of the River Forth, and quite large, over a mile long, picturesque in its setting of woodlands and hillsides. There are three islets, the largest Inchmahome – *Innis-na-Holmoc*, the Isle of St Colmoc or Colman, an Irish missionary saint of the sixth century. On it are the ruins of an Augustinian priory, the Romish successor of a Columban cashel. Nearby are the Castle Isle and the Isle of Dogs, for here was a hunting-seat of the ancient Earls of Menteith: the delightful shrine-effigy on the tomb of one of them, Walter Stewart, with his Countess's arm around his neck, still graces the priory ruins.

Inchmahome is comparatively close to Stirling, the principal royal fortress of the kingdom, and Bruce must have come here often. Records show him at Inchmahome on at least three occasions; and in 1308, on the 28th of September, he issued from here his first written orders on the governing of his kingdom. This was immediately after his return from his victory over Lame John Mac-Dougall of Lorn, at the Pass of Brander, and the campaign in Argyll. It is perhaps of interest that his son, David the Second, had his second marriage celebrated here in 1363.

INCHTURE Tayside
OS 59 NO 280288
The village of Inchture lies on the A85 eight miles west of Dundee and fourteen east of Perth, in the fertile Carse of Gowrie, between the Sidlaw Hills and the Tay estuary.

Just why King Robert chose to hold a parliament at Inchture on the 7th of April 1312, and just where thereabouts, is difficult to say. It was never an important place on a national scale, and there does not seem to have been any very large establishment here suitable for such an event.

There are two castles in the vicinity, the small and ruined Moncur, half a mile east of the village; and the larger Castle Huntly, now a Borstal institution, a mile and a half to the south-east; but the former was only a late sixteenth century laird's house, and the latter, though more important, again dates from much later than Bruce's time. It seems possible, then, that the parliament was held in the nearby old Priory of Rossie. The present Rossie Priory is the handsome seat of the Lords Kinnaird, in its large estate to the north. But anciently there was a Celtic Church abbacy here, which David the First, in the Romanising of the Columban Church, gave to the Archdeacon of St Andrews, to become a priory of the canons of the metropolitan see. It may well have been in this monastery that the parliament was held – although rather strangely, with Dundee's much larger and more important buildings nearby.

Again, there is the fact that it is always known as the parliament of *Inchture*, not of Rossie. Inchture could be an anglicisation of *Innis-tur*, meaning the island of the tower. It may be, therefore, that there was once an isle of firm ground in the marshlands of the Carse on which rose the tower of some major establishment, now gone.

A fact that is frequently overlooked is that Robert Bruce, as well as being Earl of Carrick, through his mother, and Lord of Annandale through his father, was by inheritance also lord of a third part of the large Aberdeenshire province of The Garioch, which lies between Mar and Formartine, an area of some 150 square miles and containing fifteen parishes. This fact had quite a major effect on the Bruce story. For it prompted his first marriage, arranged in his youth, to Isabel, daughter of the Earl of Mar, who died young; his sister Christian's marriage to the next Earl of Mar; and that earl's sister, Christina of Garmoran, taking so great an interest in Bruce during his West Highland wanderings. And it also contributed to his enmity with the Comyns, who among other issues coveted The Garioch, which was near their northern lands, especially their earldom of Buchan.

The town of Inverurie was, and is, the "capital" or chief burgh of The Garioch. Here rises in a strong position the remarkable Bass of Inverurie, a fifty feet high mound, which in Pictish times was the seat of justice, and later probably supported a motte-and-bailey castle. Thomas the Rhymer wrote one of his prophecies about the Bass:

When Dee and Don shall run in one,
And Tweed shall run in Tay,
The bonnie Water of Urie
Shall bear the Bass away.

The inhabitants of Inverurie have from time to time erected buttresses, to ensure that the two rivers do not achieve this.

Bruce must have visited Inverurie many times, because it was the seat of his lordship. But most famous is his sojourn here in late 1307, when he came north to deal with the Comyn and English threat, led by the Earl of Buchan, and fell seriously ill here, the result of the stresses and strains of long campaigning in all weathers and rough living. He lay sick at Inverurie for a considerable time, to the anxiety of his friends; but did not allow his weakness to totally inhibit his activities, for he was carried about in a litter at the head of his troops, as far away as the Foudland Hill, Kildrummy in Mar, and elsewhere, always returning to his sick-bed at Inverurie.

Here, on Christmas Eve 1307, John Comyn, Earl of Buchan, a cousin of the Red Comyn, thought himself strong enough to attack the king. But Bruce rose from his bed, declaring this news to be better than any medicine, and riding north at the head of his forces as far as Barra Hill (east of the A947 and just south of Old Meldrum) he defeated Buchan with great slaughter. Bruce's brother Edward thereafter went off to exact terrible vengeance on the Comyn lands to the north and east, in a raid known as the "Herschip of Buchan."

The king himself, encouraged and strengthened by his victory, rode on to win over most of the North of Scotland and to eject the English and their Comyn and other allies from Inverness, Urquhart and other occupied castles.

INVERURIE Grampian
OS 59 NJ 775215
Inverurie is on the A96, where the River Urie converges with the Don, sixteen miles north-west of Aberdeen

61

IRVINE Strathclyde
OS 70 NS 320388
Irvine is thirty miles south-west of Glasgow, via the A736: and stands on the A78(T) coast road, sixteen miles north of Ayr and midway between Ardrossan and Troon.

KILDONAN CASTLE Arran
see Brodick Castle.

Irvine is a strange mixture, an ancient royal burgh now enlarged as Scotland's fifth designated new town: not actually on the coast but giving its name to a great bay of the Firth of Clyde, it was indeed once classed as a seaport. It lies on the A78 coast-road, between Ardrossan and Troon, at a curious natural feature where the River Irvine meanderingly joins the wide landlocked estuary of a lesser stream, the River Garnock, with the Annick and Lugton Waters also converging.

Bruce granted Irvine a charter of royal burgh status in 1308, in gratitude for services rendered up until then in the War of Independence; but it had already held that honour for almost a century, for Alexander the Second made it one of the first royal burghs in Scotland. It was the capital or head burgh of the great lordship of Cunninghame.

The Bruce connection began early in his career, for here it was that the young Earl of Carrick made his first outright demonstration of armed opposition to King Edward and the English occupation forces. After his decision, in 1297, spurred on by Wallace's efforts, to "rebel" against the tyranny, and his specific refusal to attack Douglas Castle and its chatelaine, he collected a force of his Carrick tenantry and marched, with the Douglas family, to join Wallace and the High Steward at Irvine – which of course lay less than thirty miles from his Turnberry castle, the Carrick seat. Ayr, a dozen miles to the south, was now a major English-held base, and from there Sir Henry Percy of Northumberland, nephew of Surrey the English commander-in-chief, led his army against these insolent Scots. The confrontation which followed did not bestow much lustre on either side. Apart from Wallace himself, a brilliant guerilla fighter, the

Scots at Irvine were totally inexperienced in warfare and unable to agree amongst themselves; and Percy seems to have been hesitant and uncertain, despite his overwhelming superiority with 40,000 men. Wallace led a brilliant night attack on Ayr – which confirmed Bruce in his admiration for his abilities – but thereafter there developed a sort of stalemate, which ended in what became known as the Pacification of Irvine: a kind of truce, this inglorious episode did, however, gain time for Wallace to set out (more or less on his own but with Bruce's backing) on his great campaign for Scotland's freedom.

So Irvine's strange dichotomy was to be seen as early as this. No doubt, situated where it is, it featured much in Bruce's comings and goings, but the Pacification, or capitulation as it was more truly esteemed, made the town's one major impact on the national scene at this period.

There can be few surviving features to be found at Irvine today from Bruce's time, with so much of the old town demolished to make way for the new shopping-centre and other modern developments. Seagate Castle, in the street of that name, although mainly of sixteenth century construction, probably incorporates what was left of the original strong castle of Irvine, so called as early as 1184. It was the town residence and jointure-house of the powerful Montgomerie family, who became Earls of Eglinton. A plaque near the pend entrance here declares that the Treaty of Irvine (this Pacification) was signed there in 1297.

The lands of Stanecastle and Eglinton, to the east of the burgh, were of ancient importance, but their remains of buildings date from a later period.

KILDRUMMY CASTLE
Grampian
OS 37 NJ 455164
Kildrummy Castle is thirty-seven miles west of Aberdeen and ten miles west of Alford, via the A944 and the A97.

After the south-west, and of course the Stirling-Bannockburn strategic area, Aberdeenshire had probably the closest links with Bruce; for he inherited the Lordship of The Garioch and he had family connections with the ancient earldom of Mar, the main seat of which was the great castle of Kildrummy.

This is now a ruin, but a noble and impressive one, still capable of giving a fair idea of how the place looked in its prime. It is situated in hilly country, in the heart of Mar, overlooking the valley of the upper Don. Guarded on two sides by a ravine, it is in a strong position, and is a splendid example of the castle-building of the thirteenth century, with outer earthworks, ditches, a moat and drawbridge, its seven-towered walls enclosing a large courtyard, the great circular Snow Tower highly impressive. It is now in the care of the Department of the Environment.

Bruce came here often, all through his life: for his first wife, married at an early age, was Isabel, daughter of Donald, Earl of Mar, and here was born their daughter Marjory – indeed they may very well have been wed at

Kildrummy. Later his sister Christian married Isabel's brother, the Earl Gartnait, a rather ineffective character, and here she reared the motherless Marjory for her brother. So Bruce would be a constant visitor.

Kildrummy naturally became deeply involved in the Wars of Independence. Edward the First came here twice, in 1296 and in 1303. In 1305 he issued his celebrated *Ordinance for the Settlement of Scotland*, in which he ordered that "the Earl of Carrick shall place the Chastel de Kyndromyn in the keeping of a person for whom he shall answer." After the disaster of Methven, Bruce sent his brother Nigel, with the queen and young Marjory, northwards to head for the safety of Orkney, and on the way they took refuge in Kildrummy. But there they were besieged by a force under Edward's son (later to be Edward the Second, defeated at Bannockburn) and the castle was betrayed by the treachery of one Osborne, a blacksmith. It was said that Osborne agreed to do this under promise of as much gold as he could carry. The English fulfilled their bargain by pouring the gold, molten, down the black-smith's throat. Although the queen and Marjory got away, to be in turn betrayed at Tain, Nigel Bruce was captured with most of his comrades; and hanged, drawn and quartered.

Kildrummy had an exciting history in the centuries to follow, but that does not concern us here.

A view from the castle over Bruce's inheritance of the lordship of the Garioch, and above, the remains of one of its towers.

The very high quality of Kildrummy's ashlar, coursed masonry, emphasises the castle's strategic importance during Bruce's time, when it dominated the Mounth Pass.

Knighthood and Chivalry

The recumbent effigy of Sir David de Lindsay, Lord of Luffness, Regent for the young Alexander III, whose death without heirs precipitated the Wars of Independence. Opposite page, the effigy in its wooded setting of the ruined Carmelite priory in the grounds of Luffness House, East Lothian.

Some appreciation of the importance of knighthood and the idea and ideals of chivalry, in medieval times, is necessary for an understanding of much that took place. Knighthood meant a great deal more than it means today, when it is merely part of an honours system, carrying a non-hereditary title. It was a coveted status which had to be achieved, yes; but it carried large responsibilities as well as privileges and was, as it were, the badge of leadership. It had less to do with rank and social position than with ability and gallantry, although it was rare indeed for it to be won by anyone of very humble background and birth, conditions then being as they were. Yet earls and lords had to earn knighthoods, and some never did. Even kings had to seek knighthood for themselves before they could bestow the accolade on others – for only a knight can make a knight. In theory any knight could make another knight, but in practise only kings, great earls and leaders of armies usually did so. There is the example of an English earl who was unhorsed, in a battle in France, by a mere French squire, who then took the earl prisoner and demanded the handing over of his sword. The earl asked if he was a knight, and when the other admitted that he was not, announced that he, a knight himself, could not possibly yield his sword to any but a knight. So there and then on the battlefield, he took his sword and knighted the Frenchman with it, before yielding it up, the esquire kneeling to accept the accolade amidst all the fighting.

That story illustrates something important in this conception of

chivalry. The term chivalry today, like that of knighthood, has acquired rather a different meaning from that understood in medieval times. Today it is used to describe an attitude and behaviour, especially towards women, of courtesy and gallant respect. This was always the case, indeed – although the respect was apt to be shown to *ladies* rather than women in general! But it meant very much more than that. It was in fact the knightly code, and included not only bravery in the field or in the tournament, but attitudes towards foes of knightly rank, and things which could be done and things which could not. Chivalry also referred to the horsed knightly strength of an army – the word, of course, has the same root as cavalry. So it was Bruce's aim at Bannockburn, and elsewhere, to lure the English *chivalry* into the soft ground of the Forth marshes, so that the heavy chargers would sink in and so render themselves ineffective. The chivalry was the pride of conventional armies, and if they went down, the battle was almost certainly lost. It was Wallace, and later Bruce himself, who taught the Scots the weaknesses of this attitude, and to

The effigies of James 7th Earl of Douglas and his wife Lady Beatrix Sinclair in the crypt of St Brides Kirk, Douglas, Strathclyde.

take advantage of it in guerilla-type warfare, in ambushes, night attacks and other "unchivalrous' devices, which greatly outraged the English, and not only them but many of the Scots nobles and knights also.

This was one of the reasons why Wallace was so looked down upon by the Scots magnates in the early days of his risings against the invading and occupying English power: very few of the nobility supported him, because his methods of fighting, however successful, were outwith the knightly code. It is interesting to note that before his great victory of Stirling Bridge he was merely William Wallace, son of a small Renfrewshire knight and vassal of the High Steward, Sir Malcolm Wallace of Elderslie. But after that battle he was knighted, probably by Bruce himself, then Earl of Carrick; and only then was he accepted as the national leader, and made a Guardian of Scotland.

Also significant is that King Edward the First of England (the Hammer of the Scots as he became) was previously known as the First Knight of Christendom, largely because of his victorious leadership of crusades, when the atrocities he perpetrated against the Saracens – the slaughter of thousands of prisoners and the like – did not count as violence to the knightly code since they were against mere infidels and barbarians. Edward later grievously "besmirched his escutcheon" by his similar behaviour towards the Scots, his massacre, flayings and disembowellings: and especially by what he did to Wallace, a knight, whom he insisted on calling and treating as a barbarian, ordering the most terrible death which he could devise.

So knighthood and chivalry had its darker side, even though knights were required to take religious vows, make prayerful vigils and look upon the hilts of their swords as representing Christ's cross.

Knighthood, therefore, was almost wholly a military conception, and was usually conferred on the field of battle or in some representation thereof; "carpet-knights", that is those dubbed indoors and in non-military circumstances, being much looked down upon. The holding of land was considered a necessary qualification; in England indeed, in the Norman system, any holder of land worth over £20 per annum (in those days quite a substantial amount) was in law required to seek knighthood. This was not so in Scotland. There were other differences, but knight-service to the monarch was implicit in all lands.

LANARK Strathclyde
OS 71 NS 880435
Lanark is thirty-two miles south-east of Glasgow, via the M74 and A744.

This royal burgh and county town of the fertile upper Clydesdale early played a prominent role in the long struggle for national independence, for here, in 1297, William Wallace staged one of his most dramatic attacks on the occupying power. He had married Marion Braidfoot, who came from this vicinity, in the church of St Kentigern in Lanark; and thereafter, in reprisal for her husband's uprising against them, the English assaulted and murdered the young wife at the couple's house at the head of Castle-gate, opposite the church. In terrible anger, Wallace contrived the death of the man responsible, William de Hazelrig, the English Sheriff of Lanark, whom King Edward had actually created Earl of Clydesdale. It was a brilliantly contrived feat, and in fact marked the major commencement of the Wallace campaigns. Indeed, when eight years later, in 1305, the hero was captured, taken to London and executed, this killing of Hazelrig at Lanark was one of the main charges brought against him at his trial.

This statue of William Wallace surveys the High Street from its niche above the door of the present parish church.

In 1303, during Bruce's period of ostensible co-operation with King Edward, he was himself made Sheriff of Lanark, as well as Keeper of Ayr Castle, when a truce had been declared in the warfare between the then Guardian and the English and Bruce had taken the opportunity to marry Elizabeth de Burgh, Edward's god-child. This precarious peaceful phase did not last long, and the next year Bruce entered into a secret bond against the invaders with Bishop Lamberton of St Andrews, another former Guardian.

Edward Plantagenet must have found Lanark a highly unsatisfactory place, for in

1306 we read that Bruce's successor in the sheriffship, Walter Logan of Hartside, changed sides and joined the newly-crowned Bruce in revolt, and had his lands and life declared forfeit in consequence. This Logan remained faithful to the new King thereafter, and in fact was one of those slain by the Moors in Spain, along with the Good Sir James Douglas, when taking Bruce's heart on crusade, in 1329.

Lanark itself, however, remained in English hands until 1310. Edward the Second visited it in that year for a couple of days; but shortly afterwards Bruce managed to capture town and castle, and it was never again retaken by the enemy. King Robert, in celebration of his great victory at Bannockburn, founded a Franciscan friary here in 1314. He also later established a St Leonard's Hospice half a mile outside the town, to the east. This is interesting, for these hospices dedicated to St Leonard, or to St Lawrence, were for the shelter and comfort of lepers. Bruce is known to have thought that he himself had contracted leprosy, in his later years, believing that it was God's punishment for the murder of the Red Comyn before the altar at Dumfries – leprosy then being considered to be "the finger of God" upon a sufferer. We know now that it was not leprosy but a form of dermatitis or skin disease, no doubt brought about by all the rough living of his campaigning days; but it was a grievous burden the King carried with him until his dying day. These hospices had to be placed at a distance outside towns and communities, and were nearly always dedicated to either St Leonard of St Lawrence. The reason for this was that St Lazarus was the patron saint of lepers and the Military and Hospitaller Order of St Lazarus of Jerusalem was the chivalric order devoted to the relief of leprosy – as it still is. And there being no Z-sound in the old Scots tongue (as indicated by the pronunciation of "Minges" for Menzies, "Dee-ell" for Dalziel, "Cockenny" for Cockenzie and so on) Lazarus got corrupted to Leonard or Lawrence, not only at Lanark but elsewhere throughout Scotland.

Today only a few traces of Bruce's day remain. There is a large statue of Sir William Wallace in a niche above the door of the present parish church, but it dates only from 1817. The Castle Hill, an artifical mound at the foot of the Castle-gate, was the site of the medieval castle, in modern times becoming a bowling-green. There is another mound, called the Gallows Hill, at the north end of the town, where capital punishment was carried out. The ancient St Kentigern's Church, where Wallace was married, granted by David the First to the abbey of Dryburgh, stood at the south-east end of the old town, but is now only a fragmented ruin in a kirkyard.

Lanark was one of the original four royal burghs of Scotland, by charter of David the First.

This, the former county-town of West Lothian, midway between Edinburgh and Stirling, is of course one of the most famous places in Scotland, the site of a renowned royal palace, now ruinous, where so much of the country's story was enacted, a magnet for visitors. The handsome palace of reddish-brown stone stands high on a ridge between the town and Linlithgow Loch, an attractive and strong site which it shares with the large and ancient St Michael's church. The palace is now in the care of the Department of the Environment and is open to the public and well worth a visit. Here were born both James the Fifth and his daughter Mary Queen of Scots; and here was entertained Prince Charles Edward, during his brief triumph of 1745.

Bruce's links with Linlithgow, prior to the victory of Bannockburn, were few, since the place was always held by the English and strongly garrisoned. But if they were few, one of them was supremely important. For almost certainly here he was married to Elizabeth de Burgh, in 1302, no doubt in St Michael's church, in the presence of Edward Planta-genet himself. The situation was an odd one. Edward was wintering here in 1301–2; and in February Bruce, who had been campaign-ing in Carrick and the south-west, yielded in a general truce, and came to Linlithgow. There has been much debate about this "sub-mission", which did not last long; and undoubtedly there were many influences which brought it about, too involved to go into here. But clearly one of the most pressing for Bruce was his desire to marry Elizabeth, with whom he was in love. She was Edward's god-daughter, her father that king's old friend and companion-in-arms, Richard de Burgh, Earl of Ulster. Obviously before Bruce could wed her he must have the permission of both her father and god-father; and this treaty of late 1301 gave him the opportunity. It was, of course, a marriage doomed inevitably to great stresses and strains, since Bruce was soon in arms again against the invader. Elizabeth was taken prisoner after their cor-onation and the Battle of Methven, and held captive in England for eight years. But it was a happy marriage, as far as love and affection went, that started at Linlithgow in 1302.

The castle, for it was that rather than a palace at this stage, was much strengthened by Edward, and remained in English hands until 1313, the year before Bannockburn, when there was a most dramatic happening. A local farmer of patriotic initiative, named William Binnock, got together a group of stout spirits and hatched an ambitious plot to capture the stronghold. He had the con-tract to supply the garrison with hay for their horses, and he used this to aid him. Piling his farm-cart with a load of fodder, he had eight men hide under the hay. During the night, others got into position near the gate-house approach, also hidden. Then at daylight, Binnock drove up as usual, with only

one companion evident, and when the port-cullis was raised to let the cart in, he halted it directly under the said portcullis, so that it could not be lowered again to block the entrance. He and his companion jumped down to assail the gate-porter, whilst the eight men burst out from the hay and tackled the guard-house, and those waiting outside rushed in. Taken completely by surprise the castle fell to them. Bruce rewarded Binnock worthily for this exploit, with a grant of land and his thanks, and ordered the outer defences of the castle to be demolished, in accordance with his policy of denying strongholds to the enemy. But a part of Edward's construction, "mekill and stark" as it was described, remains at the north-east corner of the present palace – which itself dates from the early fifteenth century.

One other incident is worth recording. Edward's army spent the night of the 21st of July 1298 at Linlithgow, before the Battle of Falkirk, when Wallace was defeated. Owing to the Scots scorched-earth policy, the

English army, which had to live off the land, was on starvation rations, and the Welsh con-tingent, important because they were largely expert archers, mutinied and indeed threat-ened to go over to the Scots side. Edward's knights had to charge them and eighty were slain. The King himself sustained an injury in this melée when his horse trod on him. But whatever else he was, Edward was a stout fighter, and despite these handicaps, went on next day to victory.

LINLITHGOW Lothian
OS 65 NT 002772
Linlithgow is eighteen miles west of Edinburgh, via the A8(T) and the M9 motorway, turning off the M9 at junction 3.

A well buttressed wall of the palace.

LOCH DOON Strathclyde
OS 77 NX 483950

Loch Doon lies three miles south of the little town of Dalmellington, in lofty hills reaching over 2000 feet, partly in Ayrshire, partly in Kirkcudbright: the A713 highway passes, at one point, a mile to the east. The loch can be reached via a by-road, which turns off the A713 and runs down its western shore. The castle is five miles along this road.

The area of this remote loch in upland Carrick features strongly in the early Bruce story, almost inevitably. For it was a property of his Carrick earldom, and it was in these hills that the fugitive but determined new monarch took refuge after his return to mainland Scotland in 1307 from his West Highland wanderings; and from here he conducted the first stages of his guerilla campaign to free his kingdom, starting with his notable victory at Glen Trool nearby.

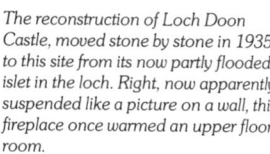

The reconstruction of Loch Doon Castle, moved stone by stone in 1935 to this site from its now partly flooded islet in the loch. Right, now apparently suspended like a picture on a wall, this fireplace once warmed an upper floor room.

He had a castle on one of the islets in the five mile long loch, but it had been basely surrendered to the English by its keeper the year before, resulting in the capture of Bruce's brother-in-law and friend, Sir Christopher Seton, who was taken to be hanged, drawn and beheaded at Dumfries. Bruce himself attacked and won the castle, but could not hold it because of its position, sufficiently near the Solway Firth to be assailed and supplied by the enemy. It was not until 1311 that it was finally won back into the king's hands.

Loch Doon has been much enlarged in recent years by damming, for the Galloway Power Scheme. Because of the damming and consequent rise of the water-level, the ruined castle was removed stone by stone from its islet and re-erected nearby on the western shore. This side of the loch is served by a picturesque by-road branching off from the A713 at Mossdale, two miles south of Dalmellington, and crossing the start of the scenic Ness Glen, where the River Doon flows out of the loch northwards – the 'bonnie Doon' of Burns' song, which flows twenty-six miles to the Firth of Clyde at Ayr, separating the Ayrshire divisions of Carrick and Kyle.

Small by contemporary standards, this Bruce castle was the scene of considerable fighting in his time.

73

LOCH LOMOND Strathclyde
OS 56 NN 400900

Loch Lomond may be reached by the A811 from Stirling or the A82 from Glasgow; and the Endrick-mouth area by the B837 from Drymen (on the A811). To get to Inversnaid however, save by the boat which plies the loch, requires a diversion from the Stirling road to Aberfoyle and then by a dead-end side-road, B829, by Lochs Ard, Chon and Arklet, a most picturesque route not to be hurried over.

As in Bruce's day, the shores of the loch are still heavily wooded in many places. It was here that Bruce endured a great crisis after his coronation and defeat in battle at Methven.

Not everyone who visits this most visit-prone beauty-spot in all Scotland is apt to realise that it had its quite dramatic part to play in the Bruce saga. Yet here came the newly-crowned but hunted king in 1306, immediately after his dire post-coronation defeat at Methven, and the MacDougall ambush at Dalrigh, accompanied by his brother Edward and his little band of closest followers, fleeing southwards into the territory of the loyal Earl of Lennox for a breathing-space before heading over to Kintyre and across the Irish Sea to Rathlin Island and eventually the Hebridean seaboard. In those days, as still today, the road ran along the west shore of the twenty-four mile long loch, with most of the east shore a trackless wilderness. So, coming to the head of the loch from the north, down Glen Falloch, the fugitives recognised that they would be considerably safer on the empty, practically uninhabited east side, for the clans on the west side were allied to Lame John MacDougall of Lorn, his Comyn-related enemy.

But how to get across? In the darkness they searched the shoreline at that north end for a boat. It was traditionally Sir James Douglas who eventually found a small and leaky craft, little more than a coracle, capable of carrying only three passengers at a time. Back and forth across the dark waters this little boat was rowed, necessarily getting the party across only in pairs, since one had to row it back. Some eventually swam alongside, to grasp the craft or oars when weary, for the loch hereabouts is over half a mile wide. Eventually, exhausted, they found a cave above the waterside and below the peak of Craig-an-Fhithich, the Raven's Crag, and hid there during the following day. This is now known as Rob Roy's Cave, and so marked on the map, for that later famous character also used it – this being MacGregor country.

It is situated in the steep wooded slope almost exactly a mile north of Inversnaid Hotel and pier (OS 56, NN 338088); Rob Roy was, of course, MacGregor of Inversnaid, so this was his home ground. A road from Aberfoyle and the east reaches Inversnaid and the lochside. It is said that Bruce, to hearten his associates in their troubled hiding, recited for them the story of the siege of Egrymor from the romance of *Sir Fierabras* – an interesting tradition to have survived, especially considering the state of mind in which the new monarch himself must have been in, having just suffered grievous defeat and having had to take a sorrowful farewell of his wife, daughter, and brother Nigel.

After resting in this cave, the fugitives were brought aid by MacGregor of Glenorchy, then chief of that clan, who conducted them secretly to Inversnaid, there took them aboard his own chiefly galley, and had them rowed down-loch to the mouth of the River Endrick, where the Earl of Lennox was hiding amongst his own clansmen in the security of that large marshy area. From here, after a short stay, the royal party was conducted on its way to Kintyre and the Irish Sea. It is said that Bruce, in memory of those fraught days, later ordered the planting of many yew trees on the little isle of Eilean Vow or Island I Vow as it is now called, at the north of the loch, and more on the larger isle of Inchlonaig further south, allegedly in order to provide wood for the bows so greatly needed by Scots archers. If so, it must have been a very long-term investment, for yews are one of the slowest-growing trees known to man – hence the wood's toughness for making bows. Today the shoreline at the Endrick-mouth is fairly well defined and the land drained, a sanctuary for wildfowl only. But in those days its great waterlogged reed-beds served to shelter a king.

LOCHMABEN Dumfries and
Galloway
OS 78 NY 082823
*Lochmaben is nine miles north-east of
Dumfries, at the junction of the A709
and the B7020.*

Lochmaben is a place which ought to be a lot better-known and appreciated than it is – although, to be sure, its atmosphere of remoteness and seclusion is a large part of its charm. It is sited in attractive country in mid-Annandale, of which long vale it is the true "capital" – an ancient redstone royal burgh, erected to that status by King Robert himself soon after his accession to the throne. It was, of course, the castleton of the main Bruce family seat, and so is indissolubly and proudly linked with the hero-king and his ancestors. Small in population for a royal burgh, with only about 1200 inhabitants, it is remarkably as well as picturesquely sited amidst no fewer than seven lochs and in the proximity of the Rivers Annan, Kinnell and Ae, so watery a place as to have been termed the Venice of Scotland. The lochs themselves are remarkable, for the Castle Loch is the home of a rare variety of fish, the vendace, found only here and reckoned to be a unique delicacy: it is related however to another rare species, the powan of Lochs Lomond and Eck further north. Not everyone, it falls to be stated, appreciated vendace; for Bellenden

the chronicler, in the early seventeenth century, writes: "Ane loch namit Lochmaben fyve myles of length and foure of breid, full of uncouth fische." But then Bellenden clearly was never there, for the Castle loch is in fact only one mile long and less in breadth, and the others are smaller still. A more favourable reaction to the fish is indicated by the fact that the keepership of the castle, after Bruce's time, carried a salary of £300 a year, a fat cow from every parish in Annandale, thirty-nine geese and specially-fed hens, and the right of fishing for vendace.

As the name implies, the Bruce castle is sited on this largest loch, on a heart-shaped peninsula jutting out from the south shore, the neck of this having been ditched by a series of fosses, which made the site almost an island and all but impregnable in the days before artillery. The fortalice was large, covering no less than sixteen acres, and rectangular in plan. Although not a great deal survives – most of its masonry having been carted off to build houses and walls in the town – enough there is to reveal something of its size and strength. It was indeed accepted as the

The ivy-covered ruins of the Bruce family castle at Lochmaben, the strongest of their holds. Right, the Castle Loch, the only British home of the vendace, a fish apparently not everyone's taste!

strongest fortress in the West March of the Borders. An unusual feature is the way the innermost moat – all the moats, of course, were linked to the loch, and water-filled – was stone-lined and used as a sort of dock into which boats could be rowed, this dock being guarded by great iron portcullises at each end below stone arches. Although there would be a series of drawbridges over the moats, obviously the castle would be provisioned mainly by boat.

During the Wars of Independence this stronghold was of vital importance, and was held now by one side, now by the other.

This was not the original Bruce castle here at Lochmaben, and was almost certainly built by King Robert's ambitious grandfather, "the Competitor," who in fact died here in 1295. Prior to this there appears to have been an earlier and much simpler fortalice on Castlehill, closer to the town and between Castle and Kirk Lochs, but little remains of this.

The town itself is pleasing, with a wide and spacious High Street. Although the large parish church dates only from 1820, it has a bell declared to be a present from the Pope to King Robert. If so, it must have been a late and very unexpected gift indeed, for throughout almost all his career the Bruce was at odds with the Vatican, and he was excommunicated for most of his reign for the murder of the Red Comyn at Dumfries.

There is an ambitious Town Hall, for the local folk never seem to have done things by half, and their municipal extravagance was notorious. At one time the Provost, Bailies, Dean of Guild, Treasurer and all five Councillors were declared bankrupt, having squandered the town's resources, and caused the corporation's revenues to drop to £10.

The aforementioned William Bellenden thought no more of the townsfolk than of their fish, for around 1600 he says of them: "quhais cruelteis wes so gret that thay abhorrit nocht to eit the flesche of yolding (surrendered) prisoneres. The wyves usit to slay thair husbandes quhen thay were found cowartis [cowards] discomfist [defeated] be thair ennymes, to give occasioun to utheris to be mair bald [bold] and hardy . . ."

Things have undoubtedly improved in Lochmaben since then.

Parliament and Government

The Scottish parliament, or Three Estates of the Realm, which survived until 1707, was a very different institution from that of England and of the subsequent United Kingdom. It was a one-chamber assembly, and was in fact sub-titled "The King in Parliament". For not only was the King of Scots entitled to be present at all sittings and take part in the proceedings; but if he was not able to be present, nor represented by a Regent or High Commissioner, it was not a parliament at all but only a Convention of the Estates.

Parliament consisted of the three estates: the Lords Spiritual – that is, archbishops, bishops and mitred abbots and priors; the Lords Temporal – earls, lords and barons; and the representatives of the shires and stewartries, with commissioners of the royal burghs. But after the Reformation the Lords Spiritual were excluded, on the grounds that the now reformed Kirk had its own General Assembly, and the three estates were reconstituted as the lords of parliament; the commissioners of the shires, mainly holders of territorial baronies and lairds; and the representatives of the towns and burghs, not only the royal ones. All sat together in the one assembly, with the monarch presiding and the Chancellor acting as chairman. So there was no House of Lords nor House of Commons.

Nor was there, until a fairly late date, any parliament building or special location. Parliaments could be held anywhere in the kingdom, to suit the monarch's convenience or the needs of the situation. Often they were held in abbeys or churches, or even in private houses or castles which could provide sufficient accommodation. Meetings were held at irregular intervals, sometimes many in one year, sometimes with lengthy periods in between, as circumstances required or made possible. Each parliament, after it made its decisions and passed its Acts, nominated a group of reliable individuals called the Lords of the Articles, who were responsible for putting the said decisions into practice and to report that this had been done (or why it had not been done) to the next sitting.

The Chancellor's position, inevitably, was highly important and influential. He was in effect Prime Minister, the office frequently being held by high clerics who were, of course, apt to be the best-educated and able individuals at that period.

As well as parliament, there was the Secret or Privy Council, a smaller group of magnates called together by King, Chancellor and Lord Privy Seal to decide upon immediate problems and requirements which could not await the statutory forty-days' notice for a calling of parliament. This long interval, not always adhered to, was to allow for members of the parliament to travel the often long distances to the chosen location. Privy Councillors were nominated by the crown, not elected.

Local government was in the hands of sheriffs of counties (often an hereditary office) and magistrates and councillors of burghs, these last usually being appointed by the craft guilds and merchant corporations, not by popular vote. Lords, both temporal and spiritual, had their own jurisdictions on their lands, as had the barons.

The judging of offences, at Bruce's period, was carried out by lords and barons and sheriffs, if not by the monarch himself, with parliament on occasion acting as a court in notably important matters and cases of treason. The professional Court of Session which (with the High Court of Justiciary) still functions, was not formed until the first half of the six-teenth century. The King also appointed Justiciars for various areas of the kingdom, to oversee the administration of justice, such as it was.

The seal of King Robert the Bruce

LOUDOUN HILL Strathclyde
OS 71 NS 608380

Loudoun Hill rises just north of the A71, sixteen miles west of Kilmarnock.

Here is a landmark which can scarcely be missed or overlooked, for it stands highly conspicuous in an extensive landscape, a conical hill reaching 1036 feet, rising above the main A71 highway about sixteen miles east of Kilmarnock in east Ayrshire.

Bruce won a fairly early battle here, in May 1307, over Aymer de Valence, Earl of Pembroke, the commander who had worsted him at Methven – and it is rather strange that he did so, for Wallace had earlier gained a smaller victory at the same strategic spot, and the veteran Pembroke might have been expected to avoid the trap. But it was in fact an example of Bruce's genius for tactical initiative and making the land fight for him.

An examination of a contour map, and even a very superficial survey of the scene from the main road some three miles east of Darvel, will demonstrate something of the possibilities. The road eastwards from Irvine and Kilmarnock to Lanark climbed then, as it does now, over high ground below Loudoun Hill on the south, through a sort of shallow pass. Drainage-water from the hill itself, and the lesser rising ground to the south, flows inevitably into this hollow and its flanks, resulting in sodden, boggy conditions, difficult for cavalry, especially heavy "destriers" or chargers bearing armoured knights. Using this feature and hiding his own force behind the hill, Bruce dug a series of deep ditches at intervals, stretching across this wet and almost level ground, but covered these over with branches and turf and bracken as camouflage. Then he led on the advancing English host by using a small Scots company, seemingly fleeing in lame-duck strategy, carefully picking their way through sundry firm gaps left in this extended hidden barrier. Pembroke's cavalry, vastly outnumbering the Scots, fell into the trap, and were progressively the more demoralized at each covered ditch; then Bruce's foot attacked, rushing down the steep hill, and *his* cavalry rode round and assailed the enemy from the firm ground in the rear, whilst the lame-ducks turned and hit back at the front. Those water-filled ditches were, in fact, only to be crossed by horsemen riding over bridges consisting of their own fallen and struggling companions and their screaming mounts – and it was only by the same means that the survivors were able to retire from the stricken field.

Loudoun Hill, in 1307, showed a prostrate, cowering nation that the English might was not invincible after all, and gave desperately-needed hope.

MAYBOLE Strathclyde
OS 76 NX 300100

Maybole is on the A77, nine miles south of Ayr: and Crossraguel Abbey is another two miles to the south-west, by the A77 from Maybole to Kirkoswald and Turnberry.

This attractive little south Ayrshire town was the "capital" of Carrick, the earldom which Bruce inherited from his mother, and therefore must have featured prominently in the hero-king's life. For it was the seat of justice for the area, where as earl he had to preside on many an occasion, and only seven miles from his main seat of Turnberry Castle. Yet oddly enough there are few references to Maybole in the recorded Bruce story; probably it could, as it were, be "taken for granted".

He is known to have come here in March 1302, however, for he addressed a letter on the 11th of that month to the abbot and monks of Melrose, who had a grange or monkish farm at Maybole, more or less apologising for making use of the grange's manpower in his warfare against the invaders. The date of this is interesting, for it was only the month before that that he had accepted the truce King Edward offered, and come to Linlithgow where the Plantagenet was wintering and there made temporary peace. There too he married Elizabeth de Burgh, Edward's god-daughter – which was no doubt the main reason for this brief period of superficial amity. So it seems that he brought his new wife directly back to Turnberry and Maybole, as was of course suitable, she now being Countess of Carrick. A little domestic interlude in his stormy career.

There is little or nothing to see in Maybole today dating from Bruce's time; such ancient buildings as remain refer rather to the Kennedys who later acquired the sobriquet of

The sedilia (priests' seats) by the side of the high altar.

Kings of Carrick, their estates clustering around (no fewer than twenty-eight of them at one time) and their town-houses being in Maybole, including the fine castle of that name, in the main street. Crossraguel Abbey however, three miles south-west of the town, retains vestiges of the earlier period, for it was founded by Bruce's great-grandfather, Duncan, Earl of Carrick, in 1244, for the Cluniac order – although most of the architectural remains, now in the care of the Department of the Environment, date from the fifteenth century. This attractive place must have seen much of the hero.

Looking through a monastic bookroom into the cloister. Below, the nave and west end of the church.

Below, detail of the structure at the west end of the abbey, and a window in the Decorated style.

Left, a late medieval fortalice tower now dominates the ruins. Below left, the remains of the abbey church seen from the high altar end, and below, the dovecot which provided meat all the year round – by papal dispensation, pigeon meat could be eaten on Fridays and even during Lent.

Melrose is thirty-seven miles south-east of Edinburgh, via the A68(T) – the most picturesque route to the Anglo-Scottish border: and four miles east of Galashiels, via the A6091.

Just why Bruce so favoured Melrose above all the other abbeys and shrines of Scotland is not clear. After all, there were other monasteries much nearer his own territories in south-west Scotland, such as Kilwinning, Sweetheart, Dundrennan, Lincluden, indeed Crossraguel in his own earldom. Yet Melrose was undoubtedly his favourite. Admittedly the monks of Melrose had a grange or farm on his lands near Maybole, in Carrick; and in 1302, immediately after his marriage to Elizabeth de Burgh, he wrote to the abbot of Melrose regretting that he had had to make use of the grange's manpower, marching them up and down the land in his campaign against the invaders, and expressing the hope that he would not have to do this again – a rather extraordinary epistle, all things considered. So even then Melrose must have been special to him.

His fullest regard for the place, of course, was demonstrated when, dying, he told Sir James Douglas, his especial friend, to take his heart out of his body and carry it on the Crusade which he had always vowed to God to lead, if He would give him the kingdom, but had never had peace to do so. On his return Douglas was to bury it in Melrose Abbey, not in Dunfermline where the rest of the king's remains were to lie, among the other Scots monarchs – surely one of the most unusual last testaments in history. He also left a letter for his five year old son David, saying that his heart was to be interred at Melrose, and commending the abbey and its monks to young David's particular care and favour. Before that, however, he had shown his great concern for Melrose when, in 1326, he allocated the then vast sum of £2,000 out of the ravaged realm's scanty revenues, for

The site of the high altar at Melrose Abbey, the burial place of Bruce's heart.

the rebuilding and replenishing of the abbey; which had been sacked and burnt by the English in 1321 at the hands of the resentful Edward the Second, in a raid over the Border seven years after Bannockburn. This Edward also seized lands held by the abbey in England. In this regard, it is interesting to note that his father Edward the First, savage destroyer as he was, had shown favour to Melrose, in 1295 giving it his especial protection and the next year ordering restitution of its properties lost in the earlier struggles. It is good to note that Edward the Third restored the stolen English lands to Melrose and granted it *his* protection, in 1328, in the run-up to the final peace treaty with Bruce.

The Cistercian abbey ruins, picturesquely placed in the pleasant little town on the River Tweed directly under the three green Eildon Hills, are now in the care of the Department of the Environment and open to the public, an ever-popular mecca for visitors. Most of the building we now see dates from the restoration of Bruce's day.

The splendid late medieval architecture of King Robert's favorite abbey of Melrose, restored at his expense following the destructive Wars of Independence. Left, fragments of interest.

METHVEN Tayside
OS 58 NO 025260
*Methven is seven miles west of Perth,
on the A85*

Bruce learned his skills in battle, especially in guerilla warfare, the hard way: for he started out no hero or experienced warrior but something of a playboy. The Battle of Methven, soon after his hasty coronation, was illustrative of this, of his inability and unreadiness to command an army in the field, and he suffered humiliating and dire defeat, a tragic start to his reign.

Methven lies on the north side of Strathearn, about seven miles west of Perth and not much further from Scone, where of course he had been crowned. That ceremony was on the 25th and 27th of March 1306. Thereafter, the new monarch quartered the land, from Galloway to Aberdeenshire, with his Queen Elizabeth de Burgh, accepting, and demanding, the homage of great nobles and chiefs, as it were showing the flag – all necessary no doubt, but probably less immediately so than preparing for Edward of England's inevitable reaction to his assumption of the throne. This was expressed by the sending north of a great army under Aymer de Valence, Earl of Pembroke, a seasoned commander, to put an end to this insolent "rebel's" pretensions, once and for all. To emphasise his fury, Edward declared that Pembroke was to "raise dragon". This was a ghastly convention of medieval warfare whereby, if a banner displaying a dragon was carried before a host, it meant that no mercy was to be shown to man, woman or child, thus giving absolute authority to an army to burn, slay, rape and sack without restraint.

Bruce was up in the Mar district of Aberdeenshire when he heard of this invasion and hastened south, gathering a scratch force, to find Pembroke had reached and taken Perth. He camped at Methven and approached Perth therefrom, actually challenging Pembroke personally to single combat outside the walls, to settle their differences – this, of course, because he was well aware that his army was less than adequate to deal successfully with the English. When this invitation was scornfully refused, and having no siege-weapons to assail the walled city, he returned to Methven. There some of his force went out foraging for food for men and fodder for horses, after their forced march from Mar. Then Pembroke turned the tables on the Scots by himself sallying out in force from the town and attacking by night. Bruce's people, taken by surprise, fought bravely but inexpertly; after all, they had had little or no experience of set battles, only of guerilla fighting and ambushes and the like. There followed what was almost a rout, and the new king had to flee westwards into the empty mountainous area around Loch Earn, Glen Ogle and Glen Dochart, with only a few hundred survivors and his queen and her ladies, a sorry postscript to a coronation.

The exact site of the battle is unmarked, but it has been variously described as "not far from the manse" and "west of the castle". This would seem to put it in the neighbourhood of the farm of Culdeesland, just south of the present A85 highway from Perth to Crieff. However, the present writer's own calculation of where the battle would be fought would be on the much more strategic ground to the north of the village, on the ridge between Methven and the valley of the Almond. Oddly enough there was another major battlefield nearby, at Tibbermuir, two miles to the south, where in 1644 the great Montrose won the first of his many victories over the Covenanting forces in his Year of Miracles.

Methven Castle, a mile to the east, set above Methven Loch, became famous two centuries later: when Margaret Tudor, Henry

the Eighth's sister and widow of James the Fourth, married as her third husband Henry Stewart, Lord Methven, and came to live here. Thereafter much intrigue emanated from Methven; and her son James the Fifth

This large town, almost a city, on the River White Cart seven miles west of Glasgow, is renowned for Paisley shawls and thread. But it is also famous as the place where died Marjory Bruce, the hero-king's daughter by his first marriage to Isabel of Mar. She was riding, traditionally on the Knock Hill to the north of the town, when her horse threw her, in 1316. She was pregnant at the time and the child delivered in these dire circumstances became the first Stewart king, Robert the Second, known later as Blear-eye or Old Bleary – this because his sight was damaged within his mother, by the fall. Marjory was buried in St Mirren's Aisle or Chapel in Paisley Abbey, situated where the south transept should be; and there is a recumbent effigy therein believed to be hers. This monument had a chequered history, being removed in the early nineteenth century by the then superior, the Earl of Dundonald, whose second wife, the Dowager Duchess of Beaufort, wanted to have the aisle turned into a Church of England chapel. The effigy was removed to a corner of the abbey garden and more or less forgotten, until it was rediscovered and restored to its rightful place by one of the parish ministers in the nineteenth century, a Dr Boog. Oddly enough, further vandalism was perpetrated on the Knock Hill itself, where a column marked the site of the princess's fall – that is, until 1779 when the local farmer demolished it, using the pillar for a gatepost and the plinth-stones to repair a field-wall. So much for the North British

called in a papal legate in the cause of reconciliation. Still later the castle became the seat of another semi-royal Stewart, Ludovick Duke of Lennox, and featured in the difficulties of James the Sixth's reign.

period!
Paisley was an important property of the High Stewards of Scotland, Lord of Renfrew, and of course Marjory Bruce was married to Walter, the High Steward. The abbey was their burial-place. It had been founded in 1163 by the first of the line in Scotland, the Norman Walter FitzAlan. St Mirren was the Celtic saint of the Paisley area, but the new Norman lords did not have any great respect for such, being Roman Catholics; and when the Steward decided to go on a crusade to St James of Compostella, he added the dedication of St James to that of St Mirren, to bring him good fortune. This led the family to use James as a favourite Christian name, hitherto little-known in Scotland; and so, when the Stewarts succeeded to the throne through this grandson of Bruce, Robert the Second, there followed a succession of Jameses. Many of the High Stewards are buried in the Abbey, with the queens of Robert the Second and the Third. The building was largely destroyed by the English in 1307 and most of what now stands dates from the mid-fifteenth century. Part of it is still used as the parish church.
I have uncovered no records relating Bruce himself with Paisley, although he must have been there often; once, of course, for his daughter's funeral. William Wallace must have been even more familiar with it, for Elderslie, his father's lairdship and his birthplace, is in Paisley parish nearby to the west. The Wallaces were vassals of the Stewards.

PAISLEY Strathclyde
OS 64 NS 480640
Paisley, now part of the Glasgow conurbation, is seven miles west of Glasgow city centre, and is reached by the A737.

The Cross Kirk in Peebles was, in late medieval times, served by Trinitarian, or Red Friars – an order devoted to ransoming captives of the Moslem infidel.

Robert Bruce, it is to be feared, could have had no great love for Peebles, attractive town as it is. Admittedly he conferred on it the privilege of holding annual fairs, and the customs thereof. But at Peebles, earlier, he had suffered two humiliating experiences. It was the seat of a royal castle, and in 1299 the Scots leaders met here, on the 12th of August. This was a sorry episode. The mutual enmity and jealousy between Bruce and Sir John Comyn, the Joint Guardians of the Realm, and between the supporters of each, flared up to the extent that daggers were drawn and almost used, the Comyn actually grabbing Bruce by the throat, and the High Steward having to separate them, so grievous had become the divisions in the national cause.

Then, five years later, in 1304, during the period after his marriage when Bruce was at a low ebb in his morale and fortunes, he was sent back to Peebles by the invaders for a surprise attack on the town and castle, in an attempt to isolate Wallace and Fraser in the nearby Forest of Ettrick. At this time Comyn had also submitted to the English. The

attempt failed, no doubt to Bruce's relief, but his mortification to be there at all must have been great.

Peebles changed hands on a number of occasions during the Wars of Independence. Its situation was strategically important, for the Forest area, sanctuary for the freedom fighters, lay just to the south. In 1301 Edward Longshanks marched there in person from Berwick-on-Tweed and took town and castle, also Selkirk, in another attempt to seal off the Ettrick Forest and keep those within its fastnesses from attacking his garrisons elsewhere. He dated various charters from Peebles, and in fact made a gift of the town, castle and mills thereof to his commander in Scotland, Aymer de Valence, Earl of Pembroke.

The town lies on both sides of the River Tweed, where the A703 from Edinburgh joins the A72. The site of the royal castle, now completely disappeared, was near the head or west end of the present High Street. In those days most of the walled town lay on the north side of the Tweed where the Eddleston Water reaches the greater river,

and the castle was on the slightly rising ground to the south. The street-names of Portbrae, Northgate and Eastgate still speak of the walled town. Two ancient churches, remains of which are still to be seen, date from before Bruce's time – St Andrew's, the former parish church, of which only the restored tower stands, was founded in 1195; and the Cross Kirk, the ruins and graveyard of which survive , dating from 1261. The old Mercat Cross of the burgh, twelve feet high and bearing the arms of the Frasers, then lords of this area, now stands in the middle of the High Street. The castle of Neidpath, then the Fraser seat, still rises dramatically a mile to the west of the town, but the present building dates from later than the Bruce period.

Left, the restored twelfth century tower of St Andrews, formerly the parish church of Peebles, and below, the Cross Kirk.

ROSLIN Lothian
OS 66 NT 275627
Roslin is six miles south of Edinburgh, via the A701 and the B7006 which turns off the A701 to the east. The castle and chapel are reached by a minor road off the B7006.

Roslin, a village in the North Esk valley three miles north-east of Penicuik in Midlothian, is famous for its handsome medieval chapel with the magnificent and fabled Prentice Pillar; also its fourteenth century and later castle of "the lordly line of high St Clair." But it had its renown in Bruce's day, for here was fought, in 1303, a most notable and extraordinary battle; and Hawthornden Castle nearby, on the other side of the steep Esk valley, provided a most unusual base-cum-refuge for the hero-king for a period.

The battle, at which Bruce himself was not present, indeed in which his personal arch-enemy Sir John Comyn the Red was the prime mover, took place on the night of the 24th of February. A large English force of three divisions had been sent north by King Edward, under his lieutenant Sir John Segrave, and his close minion, Ralph Manton, Cofferer of the Wardrobe, an unsavoury but able clerk. These divisions camped on Roslin Muir that night, presumably each grouping some distance apart. Comyn and Sir Simon Fraser, hearing of the invasion, made a fast night ride from Biggar in north Lanarkshire, nearly twenty-five miles, and in darkness fell upon the first division, in the surprise slaying Manton the Cofferer

and capturing a large number of prisoners including Segrave himself. They were then themselves attacked by the second division, and according to tradition slew most of the prisoners, to prevent these assailing their rear, and managed to defeat this force also. But this gave time for the third English division, under Sir Robert Neville, to come up, and this time it was a hard struggle indeed, with the Scots weary. So, although the enemy were again defeated, it was not so grievously, and the English were able to retire southwards for the Border. But that they were not routed and demoralised is indicated by the fact that they managed to rescue Segrave, who had not been slaughtered with the other prisoners, presumably out of the odd kind of chivalry which prevailed in those days, whereby leaders were often spared, or because of his ransom-value. But it was all a notable disaster for the invaders, to be defeated thrice in one night and by a smaller and travel-weary force of Scots.

The site of this Battle of Roslin is not marked, but since the encampment was on Roslin Muir, it must have lain somewhere to the west of the present village.
See **Hawthornden Castle.**

RUTHERGLEN Strathclyde
OS 64 NS 580620
The town lies about two and a half miles south-east of Glasgow Central Station on the south bank of Clyde, and is reached by the A749 from Glasgow city centre.

Although the ancient Clydeside town of Rutherglen, allegedly named after a Pictish monarch of Strathclyde called Reuther (sometimes identified with the individual who drove St Mungo to exile in Wales) is now almost indistinguishable from the vast spreading industrial suburbs of Glasgow, and can show little or nothing remaining from Bruce's period, it was too important a place during the Wars of Independence not to be mentioned here. It is indeed the oldest of Scotland's royal burghs, created so in the early twelfth century by David the First.

A parliament was held here in May 1300, at which Bruce resigned the joint-Guardianship with Comyn and Bishop Lamberton, because he could no longer work with the former. Sir Ingram de Umfraville, a Comyn supporter, was appointed in his place, to the further disruption of any Scots united front. Another parliament was ordered for six weeks time, in the same place, indicative of the divisions and uncertainty amongst the Scots at this period, with Edward of England invading again from Carlisle. It was almost unique for two parliaments to be held thus close in time and in the same town.

Bruce was back at Rutherglen in 1306, taking fealties and seeking to consolidate his precarious position immediately after his slaying of the Comyn at Dumfries and before his coronation at Scone. Bruce was here in especial to see Bishop Wishart of Glasgow. This was because the murder had taken place in that prelate's diocese, and it was important that no episcopal excommunication or other difficulty should be put in the way of the said

coronation, for which of course Bruce required the Church's sanction and blessing. Excommunication would undoubtedly arrive from Rome in due course, but that must not be before the crowning ceremony was safely over. Bishop Wishart was entirely helpful, in fact, urging all good folk to fight for Bruce as though on a crusade, and even presented the king-to-be with robes and garments suitable for the coronation ceremony. He actually absolved Bruce from the sin of being concerned in the death of Comyn, a very considerable help in the circumstances. When King Edward heard about this he was predictably wrathful against the bishop.

In 1307, after King Edward's death, Aymer de Valence, Earl of Pembroke, whom the new Edward the Second had left in charge of Scotland, held a court at Rutherglen, in September.

Rutherglen Castle remained in English hands until 1308, when Edward Bruce managed to capture it – a feather in that reckless character's cap, for his brother the king had tried many times to take it. Of that castle there is now no trace, although it is known to have been sited where Castle Street intersects with King Street. It was one not demolished by Bruce thereafter, but was burnt and destroyed by the Regent Moray after the Battle of Langside in 1568, when Moray's half-sister Mary Queen of Scots was defeated finally and began her sad flight to England and captivity.

The area around Rutherglen for a great distance, including much of Glasgow itself, was a royal estate, which no doubt accounted

for much of the town's prominence in affairs. The burgh's oldest extant charter was granted by King Robert the Bruce in 1324, confirming an earlier charter of William the Lyon, dated 1189.

Probably the only relic of Bruce's time remaining is a gable of the former Norman church, which rests against the early sixteenth century steeple of the old parish kirk.

The base of the sixteenth century steeple is all that remains of the Old Parish Kirk of that date. It stands to be seen in the shadow of the ornately turretted tower of the Town Hall in Main Street.

The Burghs

The burgh was a very important feature of the medieval scene. Burghs were, in the main, towns, or even cities; but all towns were not necessarily burghs and some burghs were not towns, merely villages. The burgh, however, had a status which the ordinary township or village had not, with privileges and responsibilities to go with that status. It had a form of local government under a chief magistrate or provost; merchants' and craftsmen's guilds; the right to hold markets and fairs and to exact tolls, and to exercise certain trading monopolies.

Its burgh-folk were freemen, a highly sought-after standing in the days of serfdom – indeed serfs who wished to end their servitude to their lords could "escape" to a burgh; and if they could survive therein for a year and a day, and pay the burgh's rent-charge, they became free.

There were various degrees in burgh status. The royal burghs ranked highest, deriving their position from a royal charter given directly by the monarch, with suitable prerogatives, dues and concessions to go with it, much-prized. There were burghs of regality, also with a crown charter but less lofty in status, having however exclusive criminal jurisdiction within their own bounds. There were burghs of barony, which as their name implies were attached to and within a barony, linked with a lord-superior who appointed a "baron-bailie" to act as chief magistrate. And there were ordinary burghs. Parliamentary and police burghs of course were a much later development.

These corporate communities often were walled towns; and even when not entirely so, had their gates or ports which could be shut at night or in times of stress, and these were guarded to keep out unwelcome visitors, beggars, lepers and so on. The gate-keepers could exact tolls for entry, and only allow toll-payers to come in to buy and sell goods in the markets. There was usually a High Street, with narrow wynds and lanes off it; and a Market Place, wide and open, with its Market Cross to indicate the burgh status; a burgh church; and stocks or a pillory, with "jougs" (or iron neck-rings) for law-breakers and offenders generally. Burghs had town-criers, and usually nightly curfews when all good citizens were expected to be indoors. Most had open ground, known as burgh-muirs, outside the walls for the common grazing of cattle, sheep, geese and the like. The magistrates held burgh courts and passed local laws for their communities, in the buildings called tolbooths, which usually also housed the burgh gaol. Appointment to these positions at this period was not by democratic election, but by nomination from the various corporate guilds of merchants, traders, craftsmen, millers, smiths and so on. These magistrates, under the provost or baron-bailie, were themselves called bailies. Membership of burgh guilds was much sought-after and guild-brothers had to maintain due standards of work, production and behaviour.

These burghs filled a very important role on the national as well as the local scene. They provided much revenue for the crown, usually based on a fixed rental charge for every building with a street frontage (for instance, five pence per annum for every 200 feet); and they also handed over a proportion of the tolls charged on incomers, of taxes on goods sold at markets, and on fines levied. And, of course, they provided manpower for warfare, on a recognised scale per head of popu-

The double-headed eagle, seal of the burgh of Lanark.

lation, the magistrates being responsible for seeing that such men were properly armed and officered.

Oddly enough, Berwick-on-Tweed (now no longer in Scotland because of a political manoeuvre) was the largest and wealthiest burgh in the northern kingdom at Bruce's period, it being the country's greatest port and the exporting outlet for the huge Lammermuir wool output. A year's customs duties collected there, it is recorded, amounted to the then huge sum of £2190. Roxburgh, which no longer exists, was a very important royal burgh, its castle a royal palace. Glasgow was only a bishop's burgh then, less important than the nearby premier royal burgh of Rutherglen; and others such as Edinburgh, Stirling, Dumbarton, Perth, Dundee and Aberdeen, although prominent, were less so than by today's standards.

St ANDREWS Fife
OS 59 NO 513168

*St Andrews is on the east coast of Fife,
thirteen miles south-east of Dundee
by the A92 and the Tay road bridge:
and fifty-six miles north-east of
Edinburgh, via the A90, Forth road
bridge, M90 and A91(T).*

This picturesque, famous and ancient town
at the tip of the East Neuk of Fife, being of
old the ecclesiastical capital of Scotland and
the site of its first university, is so full of history
and drama, down the centuries, as almost to
defy description. Inevitably it was as important during the Wars of Independence period
as in every other, especially as Bruce had the
senior churchmen of his day almost wholly
on his side. Bishop William Lamberton of St
Andrews was one of his most able and reliable
supporters, and Master Nicholas Balmyle of
St Andrews, Official of Lothian, a a man who
played a highly important part in the struggle,
became Chancellor of the Realm.

Before ever the real struggle began,
Edward Plantagenet of England made a
progress through certain parts of Scotland,
demanding oaths of fealty as Lord Paramount – this during the so-called Competition for the Crown, in 1292, for which he
been accepted as adjudicator. At this time he
visited St Andrews in state.

It was seven years later when the English
returned to St Andrews, after their victory
over Wallace at Falkirk, and now in very different mood, for they burned the walled
town. But the Scots won it back, and Bruce
and Comyn, as Joint Guardians, issued edicts
and warrants from St Andrews in the period
1299–1300.

Edward the First was back in the city in
1304, when the Scots cause was at its lowest
ebb, holding a so-called parliament here.

Whether Robert Bruce, Earl of Carrick was
present at that assembly is not clear; but this
was about the time when he made his secret
"band" or agreement with Bishop Lamberton, who was certainly present. However,
the next parliament to be held at St Andrews
was a very different affair, in March 1309, for
now Bruce was king and presided, Edward
being dead. This was Bruce's first parliament
and vitally important both for the new
monarch himself and for his ravaged
kingdom.

These parliaments were almost certainly
held in the great cathedral priory itself, this
being a quite normal custom in those times.
The present cathedral dates from 1161,
although of course there were earlier foundations, and was the largest church in the realm.
Something of the size and magnificence of
the place may be imagined when it is realised
that the cathedral and its purlieus occupied
more than thirty acres. The ruins of this
mighty edifice are still impressive although
scanty. The archiepiscopal palace and castle
nearby, although also founded in the twelfth
century, date mainly from later; indeed there
can be little else in St Andrews today remaining from that period. Undoubtedly the harbour directly below the cathedral and castle
was well established and important by Bruce's
time, but inevitably most of what is to be seen
there now is a renewal. St Andrews is one of
the most worthwhile places to visit in all
Scotland.

Left, the initials GW set in the road outside the Sea-Tower of St Andrews Castle mark the spot where the sixteenth century protestant martyr George Wishart was burnt at the stake. Above, the seaward defenses of the castle. Here, Cardinal Beaton was assassinated shortly after condemning Wishart to martyrdom.

Above, one of the most ancient features of the cathedral remains. Right, the spectacular setting of the castle.

The silhouettes of St Rule's tower and the east gable of the cathedral seen from below the castle site across sharp reefs of rock. Below, left to right, this view of the high altar end of the cathedral at St Andrews, viewed from the west door, emphasises the tremendous length of the longest church in medieval Scotland. A portion of interlinked arcading in the south transept.

SCONE Tayside
OS 58 NO 113265
*Scone lies on the east bank of the
River Tay less than two miles north of
Perth, reached by the A93.*

Scone (prounounced neither "scon" nor "scoan" but "scoon") is of course one of the most renowned localities in Scotland, of which it has been called the Westminster – although many Scots might take exception to that! Locality is the word, for it is a collection of items, an artificial mound, the site of a ruined abbey, a large early nineteenth century mansion called Scone Palace which replaced a post-Reformation fortalice, a group of sacred stones – and of course the villages of Old and New Scone nearby. Yet the item which has made the name most generally known is *not* there – the famous Stone of Scone or of Destiny. But that is altogether another story.

Here was an ancient centre of Pictish government – near to Forteviot, the royal residence — which later became the coronation-place of the Kings of Scots. Just when it was first established as so important is lost in the mists of antiquity and legend, but its Moot or Boot Hill was known as such in the eighth century. This man-made mound

Moot or Boot Hill, the coronation place of the Kings of Scots. Right, a replica of the controversial Stone of Scone marks the ancient crowning place.

is alleged to have been erected out of accumulated soil from all over Alba, the Pictish name for what became Scotland, the earth being brought by nobles and landholders who here had to swear allegiance to the High King, "on their own soil". To save the said monarch having to travel into every corner of the land, the soil was brought by the chiefs and landowners here to Scone, then put into their boots or shoes, and the oath taken standing thus on their own earth. It was then emptied out here, and gradually grew into this mound, down the centuries. Hence the name of Boot Hill. It is also called the Moot Hill, or "hill of meeting". So both names apply.

Here, in the ninth century, the celebrated Stone of Destiny, Scots not Pictish, was brought from Dunadd, south of Oban in the small Scots kingdom of Dalriada or Argyll, for safety from the raiding Norsemen who had already devastated Iona and so much of the coastal north-west. It may well have been Columba's portable altar, or that of some other Celtic saint, and had become the traditional coronation-seat of the Dalriadic kings. Scone Abbey thus, on the union of Picts and Scots, became the Stone's shrine and its abbot the custodian. Innumerable Kings of Scots were crowned on it. Then Edward the First of England, that power-hungry megalomaniac, deciding that all Scots kingship should be swallowed up in his English realm, came to Scone for it, in 1296. He did take away a stone – but undoubtedly it was not the renowned Stone of Destiny, which the Abbot of Scone must have hidden away somewhere not far away and replaced by a lump of local sandstone – for all the ancient chroniclers describe the true Stone as saddle-shaped, with lugs, carved and ornate, and highly polished, Scotland's Marble Chair; whereas the stone Edward took south with him to Westminster was and is an absolutely plain lump of quarried sandstone of exactly the same quality as that of which abbey and palace are built.

There is a tradition that when in 1306 Bruce came here for his hurried coronation, he was able to sit upon the true Stone of Destiny which the Abbot, his loyal supporter, had resurrected for him – the last monarch to be so privileged. Thereafter it was taken away for safety into deep hiding. The whereabouts of that hiding-place are debated to this day. Which, of course, makes the Westminster Coronation Stone, in its chair, a seven-hundred year-old fake, however renowned for all the southern royalty who have sat upon it, and for its adventures when it was abstracted from that abbey at Christmas 1950 and brought back temporarily to Scotland.

King John Balliol, Edwards's nominee before he dismissed him, had been crowned on the true Stone here in 1292; and he held his first parliament here two months later. In 1297 William Wallace and Sir William Douglas, father of the more famous Black Douglas, the Good Sir James, attacked the English Justiciar here as he sat judging Scots; he, named William Ormsby, barely escaping with his life. Bruce was here earlier, in 1299, when he and Sir John Comyn, as Joint Guardians of the Realm, issued edicts from Scone; and in 1318 he presided over a parliament here which provided for the succession in the event of his death. He held another parliament at Scone soon after the famous Declaration of Arbroath in 1320, at which certain magnates were tried and condemned for treachery.

The fine abbey was rebuilt after being destroyed by King Edward in 1298 (when presumably he realised that he had been duped over the true stone) and was again and finally destroyed by a mob of so-called Reformers from Perth, fired by John Knox's oratory against Popish symbols in 1559. Its scanty remains lie about one hundred yards east of the present Palace, seat of the Earl of Mansfield; and the Boot Hill, where the crowning took place, stands some seventy yards to the north. The grounds are open to the public.

See **Arbroath.**

Styles and Titles

A word should be said about titles, ranks and dignities in medieval Scotland, where there were certain differences from the English usage. Knighthood is dealt with separately. It is in the matter of lordships that there could be some confusion. There were three classes of lords in Scotland – earls, lords of parliament, and barons, none with exactly the same standing as in England. The earls, at this period, not only ranked much the highest but might be said to outrank their southern counterparts – this because their rank was not an honour bestowable by the monarch but an hereditary *position*. Although the word earl has a Norse derivation (from *jarl*) the position stemmed from the ancient mormaerdoms of Alba or Celtic Scotland. There were originally seven of these mormaers, rulers of the seven provinces of Ross, Moray, Mar, Angus, Atholl, Fife and Lennox. Later, with the Norse influence banished and the kingdom of Strathclyde incorporated into Alba or Scotland, seven more earldoms were instituted – Galloway, Dunbar and March, Menteith, Strathearn, Buchan, Sutherland and Caithness, making fourteen in all. These territorial divisions remained, and were not added to until the fifteenth century. Men could not be promoted to earldoms. They were in fact lesser kingdoms, the "*righ*" in the Gaelic, which means "king". Their rulers, in the Celtic polity, elected the *Ard Righ* or High King of Scots: and the earls remained a very powerful group in Bruce's time.

The lords of parliament were similar to English peers in that they could be ennobled by the crown and called to sit in the Scots parliament as Lords Temporal, along with the bishops, the Lords Spiritual. Theirs was an hereditary rank also, but their number could be added to by the monarch. At Bruce's time this class of noble was in its infancy, and many of the said lords did not use that title but were content to be called Sir James of Douglas or Sir David de Lindsay.

The third class, barons, was much the most numerous. A baron in England was and is a peer of parliament. Not so in Scotland. A baron was the holder of a barony, that is an estate held direct of the crown, not as the vassal of an earl or other greater lord. These baronies carried considerable privileges as well as rank, even the power of "pit and gallows", which meant that the baron could imprison or even hang, on sundry charges, without reference to higher authority – a considerable convenience! He could also hold markets, charging his own commission on items and stock bought and sold, and there were other advantages. This baronage represented the general aristocracy and nobility of the kingdom. Every baron had his castle, tower or fortified house, many of these being quite small. His wife was entitled to be called Lady; but he was not called Lord. He used the name of his barony; so that he might be styled just Luffness or Wedderburn or Garleton. If he was also a knight he would be (for instance) either just Buccleuch, or Sir Walter of Buccleuch, or Sir Walter Scott of Buccleuch.

The eldest sons and heirs of earls and great lords were known as Master; so you would have the Master of Mar or the Master of Crawford, not "Viscount" as in England. The eldest sons of barons were known as Younger, and still are – so you might have George Hope Younger of Luffness. Where there was no male heir to an earldom or lordship of parliament, the dignity could revert to a daughter; and if she married, her husband could assume, with royal permission, the style and rank of earl or lord, in her name, and sit in parliament in her stead.

Landowners, great and small, who were not barons were known as lairds, and used the names of their lands as their style of address, just as did the barons. They were more or less equivalent to English squires. If they happened to be chief of the name, they called themselves "of that Ilk", so that you have Moncrieffe of that Ilk or Rutherford of that Ilk, rather than Moncrieffe of Moncrieffe or Rutherford of Rutherford.

Clan chiefs and chieftains in the Highlands were in a different category altogether, of course, using the Gaelic patronymic instead of titles. The chiefs were proud to call themselves just MacIan or MacNab, their chieftains MacGregor of Glengyle or Campbell of Glenlyon. Ordinary clansmen never used the clan name by itself, but used the Christian name first, with usually a "by-name" added, e.g. Duncan Ban Macintyre (ban meaning fair) or Rob Roy MacGregor, (roy meaning ruddy).

The style Provost could be used in two distinct categories – the chief magistrates of a burgh, much the same as a mayor in England; or the dignitary in charge of a cathedral or collegiate church. The Scots equivalent of an alderman or municipal magistrate was a bailie.

A pencil sketch of Nigel Tranter's idea of the appearance of the true Stone of Destiny, which never left Scotland.

SELKIRK Borders
OS 73 NT 470290
Selkirk is on the A7(T), forty miles
south of Edinburgh and six miles
south-east of Galashiels.

The Forest of Ettrick, or of Selkirk as it was often called, played a very important part in Scotland's story, and never more so than during the Wars of Independence. Selkirk, or Shiel Kirk, to give the former royal burgh its old name, was its "capital". The word shieling means high pasture and the shelters thereon, which implies that this was anciently an area where cattle and other stock were driven in summer to gain the benefit of the lush feeding which flourished briefly on the uplands: this summer pasturing traditionally provided a period of almost holiday and freedom from normal constraints, especially for the young people.

Selkirk lies in the picturesque valley of the Ettrick Water, just below where the Yarrow joins it. It is now a town of around 5500 population, which still retains something of its old-time atmosphere, despite its tweed-mills. It continues a nightly curfew, for instance; and its famed annual "Common Riding" commemorates the tragedy of Flodden Field, when the sole Selkirk survivor from that fatal battle brought back the town banner – he is alleged to have been the town-clerk. There was a royal castle here from very early times; and in 1113, David the First established the

first of his many abbeys at Selkirk – although, to placate the inhabitants of his chosen seat of Roxburgh, it was removed to Kelso further down Tweed, fifteen years later.

In Bruce's time Selkirk was vital to both sides, because of its position on the edge of the Forest, safe haunt of insurgents. Wallace lurked here in his early campaigning against the invader, in 1297. And a year later, after his great victory at Stirling Bridge, he was appointed Guardian of the Realm here, by the magnates of Scotland, almost certainly at the abbey site, which would still be fairly entire then, and the castle. It is probable that Bruce himself, as Earl of Carrick, on this occasion bestowed the accolade of knighthood on the new Guardian.

In 1301 the English under Edward, Prince of Wales (later Edward the Second) captured Selkirk and Peebles, in order to try to seal off the Ettrick Forest; and indeed thereafter built a new castle here, presumably on the site of the old. This castle was in turn taken by the Scots in 1303. But the English won it back again, and indeed were still holding it as late as their final defeat at Bannockburn in 1314.

The sites of castle and abbey are unmarked today. They cannot have been very close

The ruins of the Forest Kirk,
traditionally the site of Selkirk Abbey
where Wallace was declared a
guardian of Scotland after his victory
at Stirling Bridge.

together, for there were originally two communities here, Selkirk Regis around the castle and Selkirk Abbatis beside the abbey, with a road linking them. It seems likely that the castle stood on the higher ground immediately to the south of the town, where is the present Castle Street leading to Peel Hill and Haining Loch. Presumably the abbey was sited in what is now the centre of the town, on its terrace above the haughlands of the Ettrick.

See **Ettrick Forest.**

Few, probably, have ever heard of this place, save the inhabitants of Strathbogie and Huntly in northern Aberdeenshire. The name, which is also spelt Slioch, is better known for the quite spectacular mountain which overlooks Loch Maree in Wester Ross. Yet here took place, in late 1307, a battle which (although on a smallish scale) was notable in the career of Robert Bruce and indicative of the man's courage, stamina and sheer driving force.

It was during his period of serious illness at Inverurie, and before his defeat of the Comyn Earl of Buchan there that, on his sickbed, he was told that Buchan's forces were massing in Strathbogie for attack. Announcing that this was the tonic he needed, better than any physician's remedies, he had himself hoisted into a horse-litter and carried northwards through the snow-covered November hills of the Foudland area to some three miles east of Huntly, the Strathbogie "capital". There, in the upland parish of Drumblade, he had his seven hundred men hide in woodland at this Sliach. It was Buchan's own territory and the Earl soon learned of Bruce's presence, and for three days tried to rout the king's forces in those woods and braes, with a much superior host. But ill as he was, Bruce made excellent use of his scanty manpower and the broken terrain, and held his positions. More than that, for although he did not actually defeat Buchan on this occasion, he forced him to give up and retire eventually, frustrated.

After this sally, the king returned to Inverurie, some twenty-two miles, to meet Buchan again at Christmastide and win a more resounding victory.

SLIACH Grampian
OS 26 NJ 555391
Sliach, which is a locality only, rather than a community, lies in the low hills just north of the A96, rather under three miles east by south of Huntly and thirty-eight miles north-east of Aberdeen, near the road-end which leads up to Drumblade. The eminences of Robin's Height and Meet Hillock are pointed out locally as the positions held by Bruce's troops.

STIRLING Central
OS 57 NS 790940

Stirling stands on the A9 and just off the M9 motorway, twenty miles north-east of Glasgow and thirty-six miles north-west of Edinburgh. The Wallace Monument is about a mile and a half north-east of the town centre, on the ridge above Causewayhead.

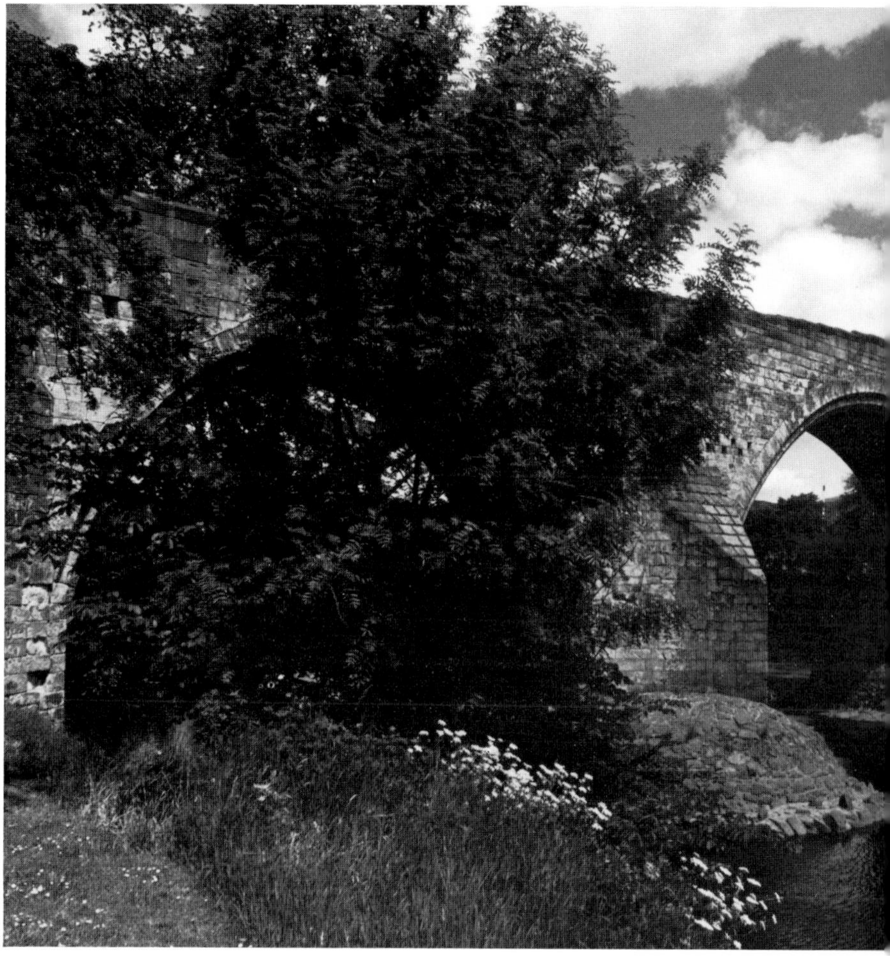

The Auld Brig, vital to Wallace's great victory over the English in 1297.

Stirling and its vicinity scarcely requires any description and elaboration here, for it is so well-known and so strategically obvious, probably the most historically vital spot in all Scotland. That its towering rock should have risen here, just above the first bridgeable crossing of the Forth, and at the eastern end of the formerly waterlogged and all but impassable Flanders Moss, on the very edge of the Highland Line, is one of those extraordinary natural features which no-one could have planned better as the very key to Central Scotland. Under that rock all who would travel between South and North, between Highlands and Lowlands, Lothian and Fife, other than by boat, must pass. And on the

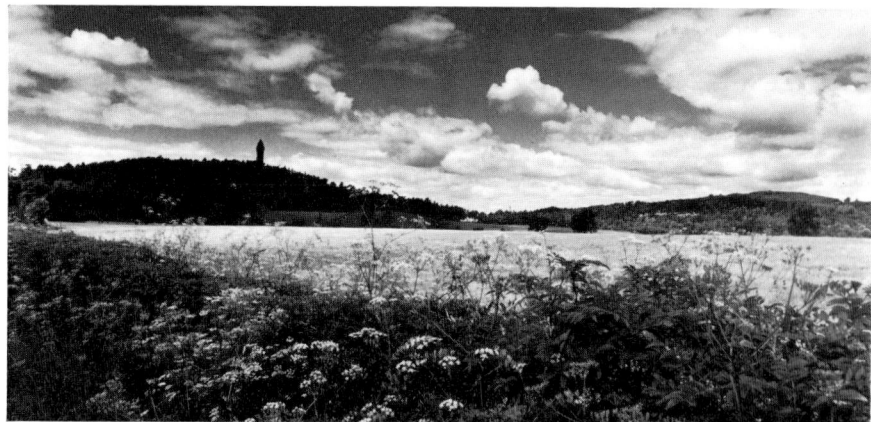

rock's summit, from earliest times, rose the inevitable fortress and citadel, to command all. The Picts used it for their own great fort, called the Snow Dun, later Snawdoun; and from that it developed into the strongest royal castle in the land and therefore the main seat of the Kings of Scots. Edinburgh and Dumbarton were strong also, admittedly, built on rocks likewise; Linlithgow, Falkland and Kincardine and others were royal palaces and hunting-seats. But Stirling was supreme and here history was made as nowhere else.

Because invading armies must come this way, if they sought to conquer more than Southern Scotland, battles almost unnumbered were fought here-abouts long before Wallace's great victory in 1297 and Bruce's triumph at nearby Bannockburn in 1314. The merest glance at the map will show the least strategically minded why.

The Battle of Stirling Bridge was tremendously significant. Here for the first time in the Wars of Independence the Scots actually defeated a major army in the field. Hitherto their successes had been in guerilla actions, ambushes, traps, surprise raids and so on, at which William Wallace was brilliant,

as later Bruce became also, adept at making the land fight for them. Here Wallace, with Sir Andrew Moray, one of the few great lords who would deign to associate with this mere laird's son, again used the land's natural features to enormous effect: and here it was that an entire great army was destroyed in a major victory, and by an infinitely smaller force. Wallace used the constriction of the enemy host by the narrow bridge, of course; but most of the slaughter was effected beyond that, for north of the river was a mile-wide belt of marshland, an extension of the Flanders Moss, before firm ground could be reached, and this was traversed by a narrow causeway. It was this causeway which the Scots used with such devastating effect, forcing the heavy English cavalry off it into the soft ground, where they were promptly bogged down and cut to pieces. Today this area is all drained and built upon. But the road-junction at its northern end, under the towering Abbey Craig and Wallace Monument, is still called Causewayhead.

Edward the First came to Stirling in 1291, in his progress through Scotland after his choice of John Balliol for the Scots throne; and in a parliament held here in 1295, the Scots themselves rejected Balliol's feeble rule and appointed a council and Guardians to lead the country instead. Edward was here again a year later, this time as a conquering invader.

In all these comings and goings Stirling Castle was sometimes in Scots hands but mostly in the invaders'. This was because the fighters for freedom just did not have the artillery and siege-engines necessary to reduce the mighty stronghold. And in the end it was this castle's position which was responsible for the vital conflict of Bannockburn. This came about in strange fashion. Edward Bruce, the King's headstrong brother, set about besieging Stirling in 1313. It was held by Sir Philip Moubray, a renegade Scot. Edward Bruce rashly offered Moubray a choice. If he would not yield then, and was not relieved by an English force in a year, then he must surrender without fighting. Moubray accepted these terms. This arrangement angered King Robert, for most certainly the English would not allow Scotland's major fortress to be yielded up if they could help it, and would send up a great army to relieve it – which would mean that he, Bruce, would have to do what he had always sought to avoid, fight a set battle against superior numbers of cavalry and bowmen. This, of course, did happen, Edward the Second himself leading his vast host to Stirling. Bruce, reluctantly but carefully, chose the Bannockburn area to meet him – with the results we all know.

Well worth visiting, as well as Stirling Castle and nearby Cambuskenneth Abbey, is the Wallace Monument on top of Abbey Craig, where Wallace's great sword and other relics are kept. It makes a magnificent viewpoint.

Above and below left, the Wallace memorial on the Abbey Craig commemorates his victory – his famous sword is on display there.

105

STOBO Borders
OS 72 NT 182376
Stobo is twenty-nine miles south of Edinburgh, via the A701, A72 and B712: and six miles west-south-west of Peebles, by the A72 and B712.

The hamlet, district and parish of Stobo, in the upper Tweed valley, seems an unlikely spot to be much involved in great national affairs. But the large manor of Stobo was a valued property of the Scots Church Primates, the Bishops of St Andrews; and being on the edge of the great Forest of Ettrick, was convenient for keeping contact with the guerilla fighters of that vast wilderness area.

Here, in 1299, after Bishop Lamberton's return from France, he provided accommodation for a meeting of the Guardians of the Realm, Bruce and the Red Comyn, and many of the great lords of Scotland who were prepared to oppose the English invaders. At Stobo was planned a major and daring raid on English positions and garrisons throughout Lowland Scotland; and a decision was made to appeal to Sir Simon Fraser, of Oliver Castle nearby, Sheriff of Tweeddale, who hitherto had favoured the invaders' cause. He proved later to be a very valuable recruit.

Shortly after this there was the famous meeting at Peebles, where Bruce and Comyn quarrelled sufficiently violently to come to physical blows. There was much coming and going at Stobo on this occasion, Bruce almost certainly lodging there with his friend Lam-

berton; and after the meeting finished, in acrimony, the Bishop remained at Stobo, to act as link with Wallace and others of his active band in Ettrick Forest. Undoubtedly throughout these years of guerilla warfare, Stobo served as a most useful listening-post.

The present Stobo Castle dates only from 1805, and is privately owned, but may possibly occupy the site of Bishop Lamberton's establishment. There is another site nearby, however, of an early medieval keep, at Lour on the south side of Tweed, which might equally be the position. The present parish church, on a mound north of the Tweed, is ancient, its tower, nave and chancel all being Norman: so that it was there in Bruce's time and undoubtedly would have seen something of the principal characters in those dramas. There is a porch with a vaulted ceiling and a thirteenth century doorway; also a rather remarkable early grave-slab monument with a very knobbly-kneed knight and his great sword. This was a collegiate church in pre-Reformation times, with a number of subsidiaries over a wide area: its incumbent was given the title of Dean, and this was long a hereditary office. Its first recorded mention is in 1116.
See **Ettrick Forest.**

Although much altered, the charming parish church in Stobo is basically Norman. Here took place dramatic incidents in the early stages of the Wars of Independence.

106

Today Stracathro means to most folk who know the place merely a large hospital, three miles north of Brechin in Angus: for there is no village or community otherwise, although there is a parish of the name and a parish church. But in 1296 the weak and unfortunate John Balliol, whom Edward Plantagenet had chosen, in the Competition for the Throne, to be King of Scots, here was forced to do humble homage for his kingdom to his arrogant sponsor: and he was then publicly humiliated and stripped of all the trappings of royalty, in the most boorish fashion, made a mock of before all and dismissed as king, later to be sent to the Tower of London – this because he had sought, however feebly, to preserve some vestiges of the independence of the northern kingdom. Even the Lion Rampant blazon on his tabard was torn off — which gave him thereafter the nickname of "Toom Tabard" or empty surcoat. This took place in the church and churchyard here, predecessor of the present parish church on the same site. There are

some very ancient graveslabs in the kirkyard which would have been there when this shameful episode took place, for they belong to Pictish times, sometimes referred to as pertaining to three Viking chiefs but probably commemorating Pictish ecclesiastics. They are coffin-shaped and no less than nine feet long.

The reason for Edward's humiliation of Balliol in this spot in an unimportant parish in Angus, was that the Scottish king had been staying in the old castle of Kincardine, some miles to the north-east – where indeed the documents of homage and submission were written out; and he was summoned peremptorily to this humble place, no doubt to make the act of surrender the more demeaning. Later he was sent to Brechin Castle, four miles to the south, en route for London and eventual exile in France. It was the reaction to this development which sparked off the uprising of Scotland against the English monarch, so that it might be claimed that it all started at Stracathro.

STRACATHRO Tayside
OS 45 NO 625657
Stracathro churchyard is just over three miles north of Brechin and twenty-four miles north of Dundee: it is reached from Brechin by the A94 and the B966 side road to Inchbare, and is one mile north of the main road.

TAIN Highland
OS 21 NH 794825

Tain is in the north of Scotland, on the A9 twelve miles north-east of Invergordon and forty miles north of Inverness: St Duthac's chapel is half a mile north-east of the town, near the golf course.

The remains of St Duthac's shrine chapel at Tain where Bruce's Queen, Elizabeth, sought refuge in vain. The chapel is in the cemetery below the town, towards Dornoch Firth.

This ancient small royal burgh, allegedly created such by Malcolm Canmore in 1057, stands at the neck of the Fearn peninsula in Easter Ross, on the Dornoch Firth some twelve miles north of Invergordon, on the A9. The name is a corruption of the Norse *Thing*, meaning a place of assembly, indicative of the Norse domination of these parts, from Orkney. This too is why nearby Sutherland is so called, meaning the southern land; for although it is the most northerly land in Scotland it is southerly from Orkney. And it was to Orkney that Bruce's queen, Elizabeth de Burgh, and his daughter Marjory, were fleeing in 1306, soon after his coronation, when they took refuge in the famous sanctuary of St Duthac at Tain, pursued by the English-supporting Earl of Ross. It proved no sanctuary on this occasion, however, for the Earl William violated the chapel and took the fugitives captive, to hand them over to the English, the women to be imprisoned in ter-

rible conditions, the men to be hanged, drawn and quartered.

The sanctuary, or "girth" to use the old Scots word, of St Duthac stands about a mile east of the town of Tain, on a mound in low ground beyond the railway and surrounded by the modern cemetery, near the golf-course; and is not to be confused with the later but still ancient St Duthac's collegiate church of 1371 (a mile away to the west) which, from the Reformation until 1815, was used as the parish church of the town. St Duthac's *chapel* is a much humbler edifice, of simple indeed rude architecture but massive walls. Apart from two lancet windows, no other features remain. It was built on the site of that Celtic saint's birth, which took place around the year 1000. He was known as the Chief Confessor of Ireland and Scotland – this in the old Columban Church – and died in 1065, his body being brought back from Armagh to be buried here. Just why the place

108

became a renowned girth or sanctuary for refugees of all sorts is not satisfactorily explained; there were quite a number of these in Scotland, but this at Tain and the one at the Preceptory of Torphichen in West Lothian were the most famous. Presumably Malcolm the Third (Canmore) came here in 1057 but it is doubtful if he came as a pilgrim, for he was anything but a religious man, despite his second wife, St Margaret. But other monarchs did come for religious reasons, most notably James the Fourth, who came frequently – allegedly to show penitence for the death of his father James the Third, in which the young James was marginally involved, and for which he wore the famous chain round his loins. It is perhaps noteworthy, however, that he only started these northern pilgrimages after he installed his favourite mistress, Flaming Janet Kennedy, with their son Alexander, in Darnaway Castle, which made a convenient stopping-place on the way to Tain – whereas his previous pilgrimages had been to St Ninian's shrine at Whithorn in Galloway, which again was suitably approached by way of Flaming Janet's original home at Maybole in Ayrshire.

Be that as it may, Queen Elizabeth de Burgh herself came here on a sort of pilgrimage in 1327, in thanks for her restoration to her husband's side and their happy married life thereafter; but on the way home she was thrown by her horse, at Cullen in Banffshire, and died.

King Robert, for the sake of his realm, was notable for many self-sacrificing acts of clemency, probably the most telling of which was his pardoning of the surrendered Earl of Ross, the betrayer, in 1309, and the restoration of his forfeited lands.

See **Auldearn** and **Urquhart**.

Opposite top, the castle tower at Douglas, and below, two aspects of the particularly interesting and well-preserved ruin of Dirleton Castle, East Lothian.

Castles

Scotland is a land of castles, probably having more per head of population than any other country, for various historical, political and social reasons. Yet visitors often remark on the scarcity of large castles, such as are to be found in England and Wales, and Ireland too. Scotland's innumerable fortalices tend to be comparatively small and very different in style from their English counterparts, with a strong French influence: and they are mainly peel-towers and fortified houses rather than great military strengths. The reason for this is fairly simple. It is not so much that Scotland never had great castles, as that they have not survived, or few have. And that is largely because of Robert the Bruce.

Scotland's large castles were mainly built by the Norman families which David the First introduced into Scotland in the twelfth century, when he succeeded his brother Alexander on the throne. He had been long a sort of hostage for his brother's good behaviour at the English courts of William Rufus and Henry the First, his sister having married the latter. He himself married a great Norman-English heiress, Matilda, Countess of Huntingdon in her own right, thereby gaining an enormous fortune in lands and money. When he eventually returned to Scotland as king, he brought with him, (and after him) great numbers of young Normans, with whom he had made friends and whose company and fighting qualities he valued. These quite quickly became absorbed into the Scottish polity, marrying Scottish heiresses to gain lands in the northern kingdom, and in fact becoming in time almost more Scots than the Scots – Bruces, Stewarts, Frasers, Comyns or Cummings, Gordons, Lindsays, Keiths, Montgomerys, Setons, Chisholms and so on. And they built their Norman-style castles here, as their fathers and grandfathers had done in England and Wales.

But when the Wars of Independence commenced in 1296, Wallace and later Bruce discovered that these castles were a menace. Taken over by the invading and occupying English, they could be garrisoned and held against the Scots, who in their guerilla-type warfare necessarily lacked cannon and siege machinery, and therefore could not recapture or destroy them. So even when the Scots did manage to recover any area, driving out the invaders, these great castles were apt to remain in enemy hands, a danger and a focus for further occupation attempts. Bruce's own castles of Annan, Lochmaben, Turnberry and Loch Doon were all thus taken and occupied, at one time or another. So it became the Bruce policy, whenever he did manage to recapture one of them, to destroy it; and when eventually he gained full control of his kingdom, after Bannockburn, this policy continued. He discouraged his nobles from building any new great strengths – and in the troublous times which resumed after his death, during the Edward Balliol warfare, this policy again paid off.

A word should be said about the great citadels, called castles admittedly but in fact royal fortresses – Edinburgh, Stirling, Dumbarton, Roxburgh and other mighty strongholds. These were not privately owned, but national military strengths, and although often damaged in war and siege, were not demolished by Bruce, since they were the seats of the kings, necessary royal palaces. They too were often in English hands, of course, and it was because the English occupants agreed to surrender

the besieged Stirling Castle to Edward (Bruce's rash brother) if it was not relieved by a certain date, that Bannockburn had to be fought, when Edward the Second came to succour it.

Certain large Norman-type castles, which existed in Bruce's time, do still remain – such as Dirleton in East Lothian, Lochmaben and Turnberry in Ayrshire, Brodick in Arran, Dunstaffnage and Dunollie in Argyll, Bothwell in Larnarkshire, Kildrummy in Aberdeenshire, Castle Tioram and Urquhart in Invernessshire, and so on, these being practically all ruinous now. The scanty remains and sites of others are to be seen, although most have completely disappeared. Closeburn, in Dumfriesshire, is one of the smaller castles of this period which remains an inhabited house

The modern village of Dunure, near Ayr, seems to shelter behind the dramatically sited ruin of its ancient castle, now sadly caged within iron railings to protect would-be explorers from its crumbling walls. The dovecot however, far left, is thought to present no such hazard.

today; although one or two, like Aboyne in Aberdeenshire, are restored and occupied buildings on the original site.

The great period of Scottish castle-building was much later than this, in the sixteenth century, when it became the policy of the crown to require all holders of lands worth over £100 Scots per annum to build "tours of fence" or fortified houses thereon, in a sort of policing role. With the vast Church lands suddenly becoming available for redistribution at the Reformation period, this policy resulted in the erection of literally thousands of fortalices, many of comparatively small size, many hundreds of which still survive as occupied houses or "respectable" ruins.

TARBERT CASTLE Strathclyde
OS 62 NR 866687

Tarbert (twelves miles south of Lochgilphead) makes an attractive centre for exploration of Kintyre and Knapdale. The car-ferry for Islay sails from West Loch Tarbert. The road from Glasgow, the A83, goes by Arrochar, over Rest and Be Thankful to Inveraray on Loch Fyne and through Lochgilphead down to Tarbert.

This castle, erected by Bruce, guards the vital mile of land between east and west Loch Tarbert. It stands on high ground behind the main street with a commanding view of the harbour.

Although at first sight or consideration it might not appear so, Tarbert on Loch Fyne, Argyll, is in a most strategic location, or was in the day of Bruce and other fighters for control of Scotland. A glance at the map will show it about eight miles up on the west shore of the longest sea-loch in Scotland, on its own little side-loch, looking across to the Cowal peninsula. Pleasantly situated, but nothing exciting about that. However look westwards, and there, stretching up north-eastwards from the Sea of the Hebrides is another long sea-loch – West Loch Tarbert. And at its head this is barely a mile from *East* Loch Tarbert, on Loch Fyne-side. So this mile of land is not only all that separates Knapdale from the great peninsula of Kintyre, but all that separates the sheltered waters of Loch Fyne from the open Western Sea.

This is highly significant. For the passage, by boat, from the Firth of Clyde out and round the famous Mull of Kintyre to that Wes-

Much of the keep is fifteenth century, it stands within earlier earthworks.

tern Sea has always been a hazardous one, with the Atlantic tending to be at its most daunting. Whereas, from the Firth of Clyde up into Loch Fyne is sheltered water all the way. Nowadays, about fifteen miles further north, the Crinan Canal has been cut through the neck of Knapdale, to link with the Hebridean Sea; but this did not exist in the old days.

Shrewd wits perceived all this. In 1098 King Magnus Barefoot of Norway, dominating the Hebrides, managed to obtain a treaty from the weak Edgar, King of Scots, which allowed him "all the land around which a boat could sail" on the West Highland seaboard. Magnus wanted long and fertile Kintyre. So he had one of his longships pulled up out of the water at the head of West Loch Tarbert and drawn on rollers, with sail hoisted and himself sitting at the steering-oar, while men dragged it and him over that mile to the East Loch. Thus he won Kintyre.

Robert Bruce remembered this and recognised how useful such a link could be in his warfare, especially in conjunction with Angus Og, Lord of the Isles, his friend. In 1316, he too dragged his vessels across the isthmus in his campaign against John Mac-Dougall of Lorn, whom King Edward had appointed his Admiral of the Western Fleet. Bruce rebuilt and extended an already existing smaller castle above Tarbert, and created the little town and port a royal burgh. Part of the town is still known as Brucehill.

The castle ruins consist of the original inner bailey of the thirteenth century and an outer bailey built by Bruce. The prominent keep is later, however, erected probably by James the Fourth, who is reputed to have held a parliament here in 1494, on his expedition to pull down the too powerful Lordship of the Isles. The building is not now in good condition.

TOR WOOD Central
OS 65 NT 840850

Torwood village is five miles north of Falkirk, on the A9: but little evidence of the old forest remains, though some ancient woodland survives around Glenbervie golf course, near Larbert (three miles north of Falkirk).

Next to the vast Forest of Ettrick, the Tor Wood of Stirlingshire was probably the most extensive wilderness area of southern Scotland, part of the ancient Caledonian Forest as it presumably was. Being situated between Falkirk and Stirling, it was a highly significant strategic feature. It covered an area of perhaps fifty square miles, mainly to the west of the present A9 highway, reaching up into the foothill country of the Touch and Gargunnock Hills, and was probably in the main not dense forest but scrub woodland territory, with stands of ancient pines and many open spaces, but also much marshland and broken ground. It was a notorious haunt of outlaws and broken men, but useful indeed for the guerilla fighters in the Wars of Independence. Wallace and Bruce both made use of it frequently; Wallace's Tree used to be pointed out but is long since gone. The wood was of great assistance in that hero's escape after the defeat of Falkirk in July 1298; and again of course in the run up

to Bannockburn in 1314, when it was in fact King Robert's choice as assembly-place. As well as these strategic and tactical uses, it often served as a refuge; and in 1299 Bruce and Comyn, as Joint Guardians, issued sundry edicts therefrom, the actual location uncertain.

Today there is little impression available of any great woodland tract, although quite large areas of trees remain here and there, with new planting, especially in the Sauchieburn and Polmaise vicinities. North of Larbert about two miles on the old A9, is the village of Torwood; and half-a-mile to the west is Torwood Castle, long a ruin but with its main features surviving, with a few relics of the forest nearby. However, this is a late sixteenth century fortalice, though possibly it was built on the site of an earlier castle. It was the seat of the Foresters of Garden, hereditary keepers, for the Tor Wood was a royal hunting forest.

TURNBERRY CASTLE
Strathclyde
OS 70 NS 198073

Turnberry lies seven miles south-west of Maybole, on the A77, via Crossraguel Abbey and Kirkoswald; and seventeen miles south of Ayr, via the A719 coast road.

Turnberry, in Ayrshire, now famous for its golf course and hotel, was the main seat of the ancient Celtic earldom of Carrick, and so was inherited by Robert Bruce through his mother, Marjory, Countess of Carrick in her own right. So as well as owning the Bruce castles of Annan, Lochmaben, Lochdoon

Access to the site of Turnberry Castle is by way of the shore from the village of Maidens at low water, or across the celebrated golf course which shares its name.

and others, he had this seat, at Turnberry Point above the shallow sandy bay of that name. Only scanty remains of the castle survive today. Built by the Celtic Lords of Galloway, it was a very ancient structure, pre-dating the Norman Bruce strongholds, but probably was not as strong as these. Like other Celtic castles, it was more in the form of a village set within a great, high enclosing-wall; whereas the Norman ones concentrated their strength on the central keep, the perimeter walling of the inner and outer baileys being secondary. Turnberry, however, was protected on three sides by the sea, owing to its position on the rocky promontory. Indeed, two crevices of the rocks, formed by the waves, have been arched over to carry the curtain-walling on the seaward side, so that the tide in fact ran right up into the castle precincts in two places. There was a door at the head of one of these, so that access could be gained from seaward by those who knew of it, although attackers there could be easily repelled. Traces of the main entrance gate-house, on the landward side, with its portcullis-groove, and the site of the moat, still may be discerned. It is generally believed that Robert Bruce was born here, in 1274, although there are claims for Lochmaben and even a Bruce house in England.

In the early stages of his campaign against the invader, Turnberry Castle held out until 1301, when it was captured by the English. And it was here, of course, that in February 1307, the king made his return to mainland Scotland after his fugitive months in the Highland West, landing by night, from Arran, and recommencing his warfare by recapturing his own castle. The English got it back again, to be sure, for it was not Bruce's policy to hold besiegable strong-points, even his own property.

What made this such an excellent site for a fortress many centuries ago, made it a natural choice for the lighthouse which stands here today.

URQUHART CASTLE
Highland
OS 26 NH 531285

Urquhart Castle stands on the north shore of Loch Ness, and by the main A82, sixteen miles south-west of Inverness.

Visitors to Loch Ness, hoping to catch a glimpse of the elusive Monster, could do a lot worse than spend some time viewing a more reliable feature there, Urquhart Castle, on the north shore of the loch – itself as good a place as any to look for the creature. It stands on a rocky promontory, on the site of an early Pictish fort where, in the late sixth century, St Columba himself baptised a Pictish chieftain called Emchath and his son Virolec – and where one of the saint's Celtic monks is recorded as having had a narrow escape from what was then called the *aquatilis bestia*, the Beast of the Loch.

There was a royal castle on this strategic spot from the twelfth century reign of William the Lion, for it marked the boundary between the great provinces of Moravia (or Moray) and Ergadia (or Argyll). It was, like so many others, taken and occupied by the English in the Wars of Independence and was captured and recaptured two or three times. After a stubborn defence in the Scots interest, in 1303, by Sir Alexander Forbes, Sir Alexander Comyn, a kinsman of the Red Comyn, then

supporting the English side, was appointed Constable; and in 1308 Bruce himself came to besiege it, as part of his campaign against William, Earl of Ross, who also supported the English. Bruce was successful both in reducing the castle and in bringing down the Earl; and thereafter followed his famous act of forgiveness to that treacherous chief, who had betrayed Bruce's queen and daughter to the English at Tain. Later, in 1313, the King granted Urquhart to his nephew, Thomas Randolph, whom he created Earl of Moray, and who was to become Regent of Scotland for the young David the Second, Bruce's infant successor.

The castle is extensive and much of it remains, its ruins reaching over 500 feet within its curtain-walls and behind its drawbridge ditch. The oldest part would be the Norman motte on the higher rock-platform at the west end, which also was the site of the Pictish fort. Parts of the curtain-walling facing the loch are also part of the building of Bruce's time, but most of the present ruins date from major rebuilding in 1509.

Left, a pile of catapult stones as used by the siege engines of Bruce's day stands by the entrance to the castle. Above, the Norman motte is probably the oldest part of the site. The castle was captured by Bruce and largely demolished by him in keeping with his policy of leaving no stone castles intact for his enemies to recapture and defend again to his cost.

119

WHITHORN Dumfries and
Galloway
OS 83 NX 444403 (Priory)
481363 (St Ninian's Chapel)
*Whithorn is twelve miles south of
Wigtown, by the A746: Isle of
Whithorn village, and St Ninian's
chapel, are a further three miles
south-east of Whithorn, via the A750.*

This small town, with its ancient Priory, and
the still more ancient small ruined chapel of
St Ninian at Isle of Whithorn some three
miles further south, is at the very tail-end of
Scotland, the extreme southern tip of the
central peninsula of Galloway – indeed Isle
is the most southerly village in Scotland. And
it was at the latter end of Bruce's career and
life that he came here, indeed the last journey
that he made. Like all else, it was for a purpose, an indomitable purpose. He came here
in 1329 from Cardross in the Lennox, on a
pilgrimage — for this was, and still is for
some, a place of pilgrimage, and long may
it remain so. Here Christianity first came to
Scotland, in any sustained mission, brought
by St Ninian at the end of the fourth century.
Ninian, a Celt of probably royal descent, is
thought to have been born hereabouts but
journeyed to Rome, was consecrated bishop
by the Pope and returned to preach the faith
of Christ crucified and convert his fellow-
countrymen. He seems first to have established himself in a sea-shore cave about a
mile to the south-west of the village of Isle,
but later erected a humble chapel on the little
headland near the harbour, which he called
Candida Casa, or the White House, this in
A.D. 397 The present chapel, known as
St Ninian's Kirk, is probably built on the same
site but is not the original shrine, although it
is a very early edifice.

From here Ninian set out to spread the
message of the Gospel, first to his fellow-
Gallovidians and then to the Picts or
Cruithne, at large, for the Scots had not yet
come from Ireland. That he did not succeed,
or at least that such success as he achieved
did not last, was not Ninian's fault. It was left
to the Scots-Irish Columba, a century and a
half later, to establish Christianity in this land,
from famed Iona. But Ninian was the first.

Quite early on thereafter Whithorn
became a place of pilgrimage, and remained
so; at the Reformation, indeed, the continu-
ance of this so-called Popish superstition so
worried the reformers that they actually had
the custom put down by act of parliament in
1581. By that time, of course, the centre of
worship and depository of relics had moved
to Whithorn town itself, where was established the renowned Priory, built in the twelfth
and fifteenth centuries, the church of which
became the cathedral of the Bishops of Galloway. This interesting edifice is reached from
an arched pend on the west side of Whithorn
High Street, under a fine heraldic panel displaying the royal arms of Scotland.

If Ninian's was a hard fight, so was Robert
Bruce's, all the days of his struggle, from
1296 until 1329, when he came here in the
last months of his life. It must have made a
sore journey for a man dying of dropsy and
weakened by all the years of campaigning. He
had only the previous year won his long
sought – for peace-treaty with England. He
was in fact bedbound, and had to be carried
in a horse-litter all the weary miles from the

This chapel at Isle of Whithorn served pilgrims journeying to St Ninian's shrine.

skirts of the Highlands, to the greatest taxing of his failing strength. Indeed it is sometimes averred that he made the journey deliberately to hasten his death, since he knew that there was no recovery and he was impatient to rejoin his wife and queen, Elizabeth de Burgh, who had died two years before whilst herself on a pilgrimage to St Duthac's shrine at Tain in Ross.

Bruce was a man with a conscience and a very active one, uncomfortably so. He had slain the Red Comyn with his dirk at the altar of the Greyfriars Kirk at Dumfries, twenty-three years before, and however justified that treacherous man's death, the killer never forgot it and believed that his Maker would not forget it either, however much he might repent of it. He had had but little time and

Whithorn Priory, to which Bruce made pilgrimage.

opportunity for repentant pilgrimages in his long years of continuing warfare. Whether he had ever come to Whithorn previously we do not know; but belatedly he made this journey now, to the shrine of another heroic and lonely figure of south-west Scotland, who had fought for Christ's kingdom rather than his own.

Both the priory and the older chapel are picturesque and worth seeing, visited by many other distinguished pilgrims down the ages, notably James the Fourth, who came here many times. The famous James Beaton, later Archbishop of St Andrews and Primate and Chancellor of Scotland, was Prior here in his earlier days.

The Rivals for the Thron

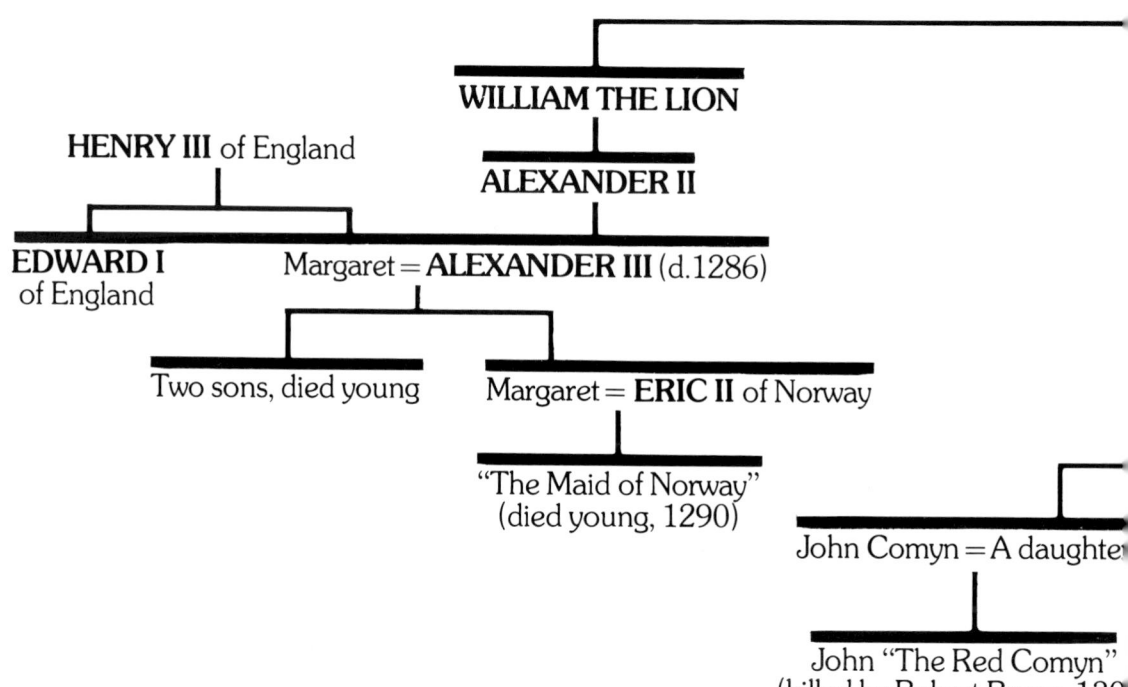

WILLIAM THE LION

HENRY III of England

ALEXANDER II

EDWARD I
of England

Margaret = **ALEXANDER III** (d.1286)

Two sons, died young

Margaret = **ERIC II** of Norway

"The Maid of Norway"
(died young, 1290)

John Comyn = A daughter

John "The Red Comyn"
(killed by Robert Bruce, 130

This tree sets out the dilemma which faced Scotland after the sudden death of King Alexander III. His only direct descendant was the little "Maid of Norway" and when she too died, the throne was disputed between his distant relations, the heirs of David Earl of Huntingdon. Who should succeed, John Balliol or Robert Bruce "the Competitor"? Balliol was the grandson of Margaret, Earl David's eldest daughter: while Bruce, though his claim was derived only from the second daughter Isabel, was

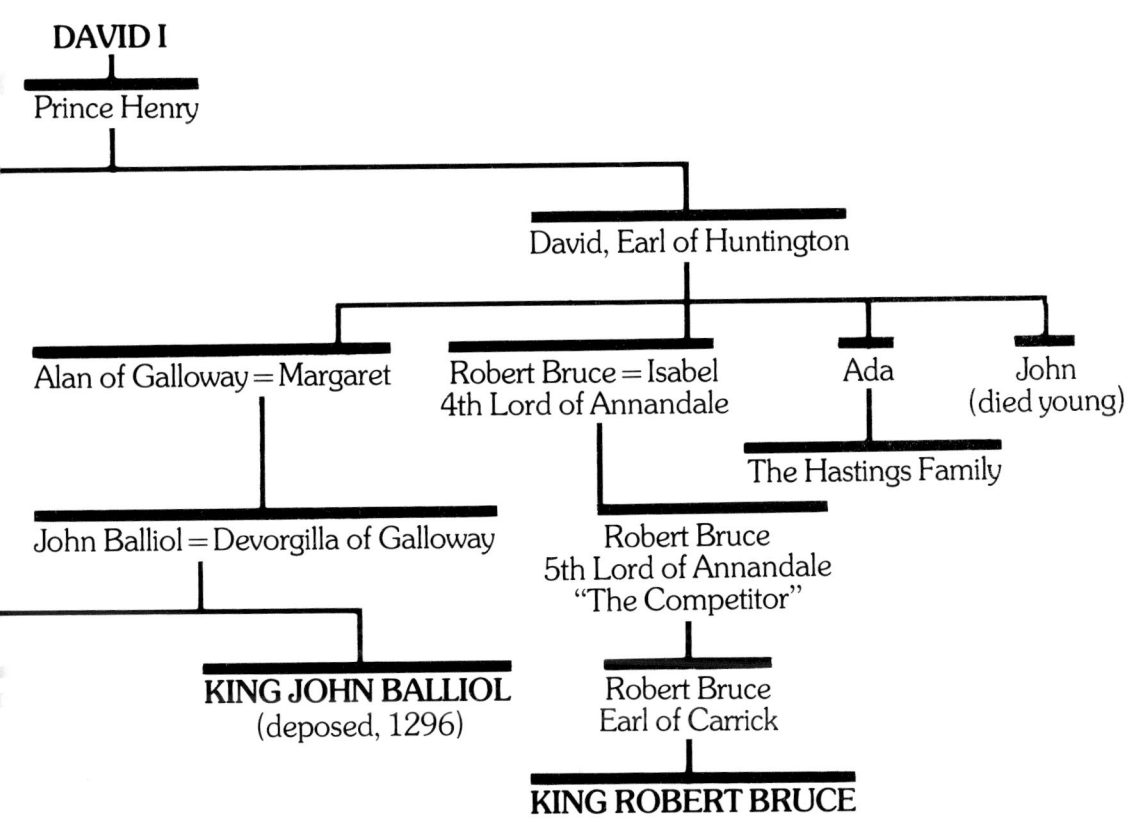

DAVID I
Prince Henry

David, Earl of Huntington

Alan of Galloway = Margaret   Robert Bruce = Isabel   Ada   John
                               4th Lord of Annandale   (died young)

                                                        The Hastings Family

John Balliol = Devorgilla of Galloway   Robert Bruce
                                         5th Lord of Annandale
                                         "The Competitor"

KING JOHN BALLIOL   Robert Bruce
(deposed, 1296)   Earl of Carrick

                                   KING ROBERT BRUCE

one generation nearer the source, for he was Isabel's son. Both Balliol and Bruce took up arms and gathered their supporters, and in order to prevent a civil war King Edward of England—who had a claim of his own—was called on to decide between them. He chose Balliol, only to depose him in 1296 and take Scotland for himself: but then "the Competitor's" grandson, the young Robert Bruce, took a hand, slaying John Comyn and seizing the throne in 1306.

A Pride of Bruces

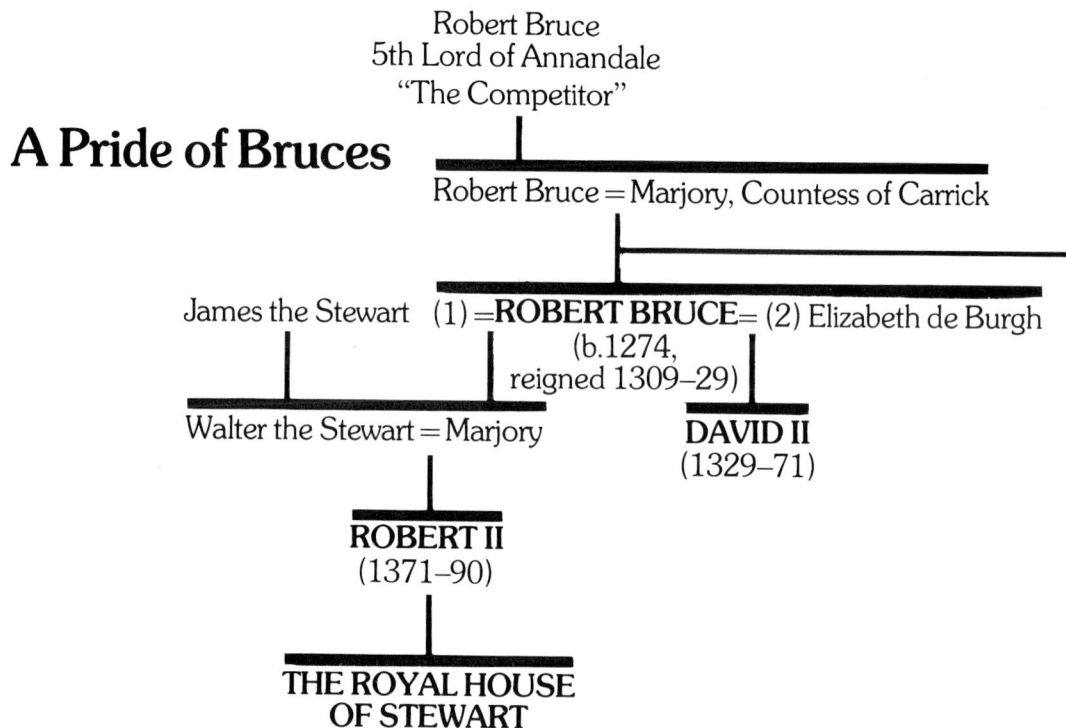

Robert Bruce
5th Lord of Annandale
"The Competitor"

Robert Bruce = Marjory, Countess of Carrick

James the Stewart   (1) = **ROBERT BRUCE** = (2) Elizabeth de Burgh
(b.1274,
reigned 1309–29)

Walter the Stewart = Marjory   **DAVID II**
(1329–71)

ROBERT II
(1371–90)

**THE ROYAL HOUSE
OF STEWART**

Here are set out the family connections of the hero-king. From his grandfather he inherited Annadale, and from his mother the lordship of Carrick: while through the marriages of his sister Christian he gained the support of the powerful Mar family and of Sir Christopher Seton. His daughter Marjory's marriage, moreover, strengthened Bruces alliance with James the Stewart: and from her descended the royal house of Stewart, who (after the death of the king's son David) were to rule first Scotland and eventually all Britain.

Edward Bruce
(d.1318)

Nigel Bruce
(hanged by the English 1306)

Christian Bruce
m. (1) Gartnait, Earl of Mar
(2) Sir Christopher Seton,
(hanged by the English 1306)

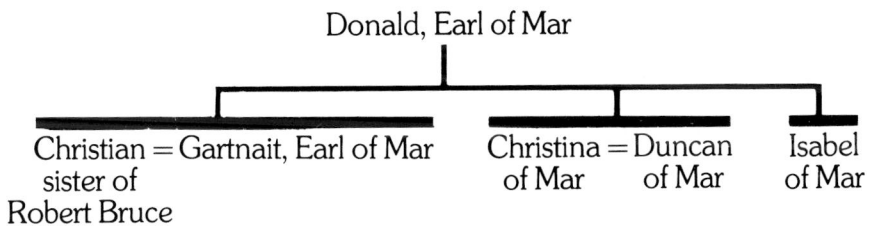

Donald, Earl of Mar

Christian = Gartnait, Earl of Mar
sister of
Robert Bruce

Christina = Duncan
of Mar   of Mar

Isabel
of Mar

FURTHER READING

Anderson, A. O., *Early Sources of Scottish History,* Edinburgh, 1922
Barbour, J., *The Bruce* (ed. W. M. Mackenzie), London, 1909
Barrow, G. W. S., *Robert Bruce,* London, 1965
Barrow, G. W. S., *The Kingdom of the Scots,* London, 1973
'Blind Hary', *Wallace* (ed. M. P. McDiarmid), Scottish Text Society, Edinburgh, 1968–9
Chambers, R., *Biographical Dictionary of Eminent Scotsmen,* Edinburgh, 1852
Dunbar, A. H., *Scottish Kings,* Edinburgh, 1906
Fraser-Tytler, P., *History of Scotland,* Edinburgh, 1879
Grub, G., *Ecclesiastical History of Scotland,* Edinburgh, 1861
Harvey, J., *Life of Robert Bruce,* Edinburgh, 1818
Hill Burton, J., *History of Scotland,* Edinburgh, 1867
Nicholson, R., *Scotland – The Later Middle Ages,* Edinburgh, 1974